Everything you need to know about FE Policy

Other Titles in the Essential FE Toolkit Series

Books for Lecturers

Teaching the FE Curriculum – Mark Weyers

e-Learning in FE – John Whalley, Theresa Welch and Lee Williamson

FE Lecturer's Survival Guide – Angela Steward

FE Lecturer's Guide to Diversity and Inclusion – Anne-Marie Wright, Sue Colquhoun, Sina Abdi-Jama, Jane Speare and Tracey Partridge

How to Manage Stress in FE – Elizabeth Hartney

Guide to Teaching 14–19 – James Ogunleye

Ultimate FE Lecturer's Handbook – Ros Clow and Trevor Dawn

A to Z of Teaching in FE – Angela Steward

Getting the Buggers Motivated in FE – Sue Wallace

Books for Managers

Middle Management in FE – Ann Briggs

Managing Higher Education in Colleges – Gareth Parry, Anne Thompson and Penny Blackie

Survival Guide for College Managers and Leaders – David Collins

Guide to Leadership and Governance in FE – Adrian Perry

Guide to Financial Management in FE – Julian Gravatt

Guide to Race Equality in FE – Beulah Ainley

Ultimate FE Leadership and Management Handbook – Jill Jameson and Ian McNay

A to Z for Every Manager in FE – Susan Wallace and Jonathan Gravells

Guide to VET – Christopher Winch and Terry Hyland

Everything you need to know about FE policy

Yvonne Hillier

continuum

Continuum International Publishing Group

The Tower Building   80 Maiden Lane, Suite 704
11 York Road   New York
London   NY 10038
SE1 7NX

British Library Cataloguing-in-Publication Data
A catalogue record for this book is available from the British Library.

ISBN: 0–8264–8807–2 (paperback)

Library of Congress Cataloging-in-Publication Data
A catalog record for this book is available from the Library of Congress.

Typeset by YHT Ltd, London
Printed and bound in Great Britain by Ashford Colour Press, Gosport, Hampshire

Contents

Series Foreword   ix
Series Introduction   xiii
Acknowledgements   xv
Introduction   xvi

1 **So what is policy? Definitions and analyses**   **1**
   Rational policymaking   3
   Criticisms of any policy analysis approach   12
   Policy analysis in practice   13
   Critically reflective approaches to FE policy   16
2 **A recent history of post-compulsory policy
   from 1944**   **20**
   A 'pre-history' of further education   21
   A sector becomes institutionalized   22
   The 1970s   23
   The 1980s   25
   The 1990s   27
   From competition to collaboration   30
   2000 – another decade, another change   32
3 **Success for All**   **35**
   The Learning and Skills Act   36
   FE and Centres for Vocational Excellence   37
   Success for All   38
   Realising our Potential   41
   Targets, targets, targets   46
   Policy analysis of Success for All   48
   So what does this mean for a college manager?   49
4 **Skills for Life**   **51**
   Policy analysis of Skills for Life   59
   The impact of Skills for Life   60

	Yes, but is it working?	62
	What does Skills for Life mean for managers?	63
	How to keep informed	64
5	**A question of qualifications**	**66**
	The story begins	67
	Working with the unqualified	69
	Tinkering with A levels	71
	The Tomlinson Review	71
	Framework for Achievement (FfA)	75
	Wider education policy	77
	What does this mean for managers?	79
6	**Assuring quality**	**81**
	Who is responsible for quality?	82
	A common approach to assuring quality?	83
	A national quality improvement body	87
	Joined-up enhancement: the role of staff in the sector	89
	Policy analysis of quality	92
7	**Moving forward**	**95**
	Ongoing and new initiatives	95
	Overarching issues	96
	Challenges, opportunities and change	101
	Staff in the sector	103
	How have we done so far?	104
	Back to the future	108
	Postscript	110
	Glossary and useful acronyms	112
	Useful websites	115
	Bibliography	117
	Index	127

For my father

Series foreword

THE ESSENTIAL FE TOOLKIT SERIES

Jill Jameson
Series Editor

*In the autumn of 1974, a young woman newly arrived from Africa
landed in Devon to embark on a new life in England. Having
travelled half way round the world, she still longed for sunny
Zimbabwe. Not sure what career to follow, she took a part-time job
teaching EFL to Finnish students. Having enjoyed this, she studied
thereafter for a PGCE at the University of Nottingham in Ted
Wragg's Education Department. After teaching in secondary schools,
she returned to university in Cambridge, and, after graduating, took
a job in ILEA in 1984 in adult education. She loved it: there was
something about adult education that woke her up, made her feel
fully alive, newly aware of all the lifelong learning journeys being
followed by so many students and staff around her. The adult
community centre she worked in was a joyful place for diverse multi-
ethnic communities. Everyone was cared for, including 90-year-olds
in wheelchairs, toddlers in the crèche, ESOL refugees, city account-
ants in business suits and university level graphic design students. In
her eyes, the centre was an educational ideal, a remarkable place in
which, gradually, everyone was helped to learn to be who they
wanted to be. This was the Chequer Centre, Finsbury, EC1, the
'red house', as her daughter saw it, toddling in from the crèche. And
so began the story of a long interest in further education that was to
last for many years . . . why, if they did such good work for so many,
were FE centres so under-funded and unrecognized, so under-
appreciated?*

It is with delight that, 32 years after the above story began, I
write the Foreword to *The Essential FE Toolkit*, Continuum's
new series of 24 books on further education (FE) for teachers
and college leaders. The idea behind the *Toolkit* is to provide a

comprehensive guide to FE in a series of compact, readable books. The suite of 24 individual books are gathered together to provide the practitioner with an overall FE toolkit in specialist, fact-filled volumes designed to be easily accessible, written by experts with significant knowledge and experience in their individual fields. All of the authors have in-depth understanding of further education. But 'Why is further education important? Why does it merit a whole series to be written about it?' you may ask.

At the Association of Colleges Annual Conference in 2005, in a humorous speech to college principals, John Brennan said that, whereas in 1995 further education was a 'political backwater', by 2005 it had become 'mainstream'. John recalled that since 1995 there had been '36 separate Government or Government-sponsored reports or white papers specifically devoted to the post-16 sector'. In our recent regional research report (2006) for the Learning and Skills Development Agency, my co-author Yvonne Hillier and I noted that it was no longer 'raining policy' in FE, as we had described earlier (Hillier and Jameson, 2003): there is now a torrent of new initiatives. We thought in 2003 that an umbrella would suffice to protect you. We'd now recommend buying a boat to navigate these choppy waters, as it looks as if John Brennan's 'mainstream' FE, combined with a tidal wave of government policies, will soon lead to a flood of new interest in the sector, rather than end anytime soon.

There are good reasons for all this government attention on further education. In 2004/2005, student numbers in LSC-funded further education increased to 4.2m, total college income was around £6.1 billion, and the average college had an annual turnover of £15m. Further education has rapidly increased in national significance regarding the need for ever greater achievements in UK education and skills training for millions of learners, providing qualifications and workforce training to feed a UK national economy hungrily in competition with other OECD nations. The 120 recommendations of the Foster Review (2005) therefore in the main encourage colleges to focus their work on vocational skills, social inclusion and achieving academic progress. This series is here to consider all three of these areas and more.

The series is written for teaching practitioners, leaders and managers in the 572 FE/LSC-funded institutions in the UK, including FE colleges, adult education and sixth form institutions, prison education departments, training and workforce development units, local education authorities and community agencies. The series is also written for PGCE/Cert Ed/City & Guilds Initial and continuing professional development (CPD) teacher trainees in universities in the UK, USA, Canada, Australia, New Zealand and beyond. It will also be of interest to staff in the 600 Jobcentre Plus providers in the UK and to many private training organizations. All may find this series of use and interest in learning about FE educational practice in the 24 different areas of these specialist books from experts in the field.

Our use of this somewhat fuzzy term 'practitioners' includes staff in the FE/LSC-funded sector who engage in professional practice in governance, leadership, management, teaching, training, financial and administration services, student support services, ICT and MIS technical support, librarianship, learning resources, marketing, research and development, nursery and crèche services, community and business support, transport and estates management. It is also intended to include staff in a host of other FE services including work-related training, catering, outreach and specialist health, diagnostic additional learning support, and pastoral and religious support for students. Updating staff in professional practice is critically important at a time of such continuing radical policy-driven change, and we are pleased to contribute to this nationally and internationally.

We are also privileged to have an exceptional range of authors writing for the series. Many of our series authors are renowned for their work in further education, having worked in the sector for thirty years or more. Some have received OBE or CBE honours, professorships, fellowships and awards for contributions they have made to further education. All have demonstrated a commitment to FE that makes their books come alive with a kind of wise guidance for the reader. Sometimes this is tinged with world-weariness, sometimes with sympathy, humour or excitement. Sometimes the books are just plain clever or a fascinating read, to guide practitioners of the future who will read these works. Together, the books make up a considerable portfolio of assets for you to take with you through your journeys in further education. We hope the experience of reading the books will be interesting, instructive and pleasurable and that experience gained from them will last, renewed, for many seasons.

It has been wonderful to work with all of the authors and with Continuum's UK Education Publisher, Alexandra Webster, on this series. The exhilarating opportunity of developing such a comprehensive toolkit of books probably comes once in a lifetime, if at all. I am privileged to have had this rare opportunity, and I thank the publishers, authors and other contributors to the series for making these books come to life with their fantastic contributions to FE.

Dr Jill Jameson
Series Editor
March, 2006

Series Introduction

**Everything you need to know about FE policy –
Professor Yvonne Hillier**

Have you ever been completely bewildered by the number of
policy developments in further education? In November, 1995,
in his speech to the tenth Annual Conference of the Association
of Colleges (AoC), John Brennan, CEO of the AoC, reminded
us that there were 36 different government or government-
funded reports or white papers on policy initiatives in the post-
16 sector during 1995–2005. This tidal wave of policies can be
disorientating for those already in or entering into FE
employment. How do you make sense of all of these policies?
How can you put them into context for the longer term so that
it all makes sense?

Here is an unusual book that will help you do just that.
Professor Yvonne Hillier, widely acknowledged expert on
post-compulsory education and Chair of Education at Brighton
University, has written a delightfully accessible, friendly and
practical policy guide for managers and practitioners to help us
grapple with the fast-changing world of further education
policy developments. Yvonne defines public policy analysis,
methods and theories overall and provides a history of policy on
further education from 1944–2006. She examines in depth a
range of different policy initiatives from 1992–2006, including
Success for All, Skills for Life, the new *Qualifications Framework* for
14–19 education and the *Tomlinson Report*, and a range of
important quality documents including the *Common Inspection
Framework*. Yvonne briefly describes the impact of the 2005
Foster Report and the 2006 White Paper on FE, providing
us with a comprehensive range of references for further information and specialist advice to take forward in the future. She

provides us with numerous useful suggestions to help us grapple more confidently with potential new FE policy reforms in the future.

In each main chapter, Yvonne discusses the implications of implementing policy in institutions, describing ways to manage change and work with staff effectively to achieve policy aims. As all policy initiatives are fast changing, Yvonne advises us to adopt a critical, informed and reflective approach to new policies. She suggests we put all policy changes into a deeper, longer-term context: whether and how such policies are significant for the people who matter most in FE – the students and teachers. This brilliant guide will tell you everything you need to know about policy in FE and help you to apply it in practice as well!

Dr Jill Jameson
Director of Research
School of Education and Training
University of Greenwich
j.jameson@gre.ac.uk

Acknowledgements

I would like to thank Jill Jameson for her outstanding work as editor of the Toolkit for FE Managers Series. She has worked tirelessly and enthusiastically to ensure that all authors are able to meet her schedule and, more importantly, to meet each other and feel part of a community of practice. Thanks, too, to my husband, John Pratt, who often has the source or reference I need to consult, as well as introducing me, a long time ago, to policy analysis and its importance. Thanks to Alexandra Webster, for her continuing support for my writing, and her kind words which help keep me on task. Thanks to Mike Cooper, Trixi Blaire and my colleagues at the Learning and Skills Research Network who keep me up to date with current events, particularly helping me to understand what it feels like to be implementing policy as well as critiquing it. Here's to the future of networking amongst practitioners and managers in the further education sector.

Yvonne Hillier
February 2006

Introduction

It is impossible to keep up with the number of policies that emanate from the United Kingdom Government these days. By the time you read these pages, some of the contents will be out of date, superseded by new initiatives, new imperatives and a rejection of existing ideas and activities. People who are managers in further education (FE), adult and community learning (ACL) or higher education (HE) know this only too well, simply by observing the number of documents that arrive on their desks each week.

The purpose of this book, then, is to enable people to use strategies to manage this policy overload. The most important tool in achieving this is understanding what policymaking is and how it can be analysed. Rather than be the unwitting recipients of policy from above (e.g. from national government, local and regional agencies), I hope that readers will begin to take more control of their situation by being able to engage in an informed manner with the implementation of policies.

It would be naive to assume that knowing where a policy comes from will ensure that it is enacted upon in ways to achieve its outcomes or that its consequences will be less damaging to its target audiences. Managers are small components of an extremely large infrastructure of learning providers in the country. However, not doing anything is more dangerous. Policies can and should attempt to address the fundamental aims of enabling as many people as possible to learn effectively and achieve their personal, civic and economic goals.

I hope that a deeper knowledge of the policy framework in which FE is placed will enable managers to act wisely, critically and effectively.

1 So what is policy? Definitions and analyses

> 'Public policy is really about defining what counts as public, who provides, who pays, how they pay and who they pay.' (Parsons 1995: 11)

Most people use the word 'policy' as shorthand for all sorts of activities. They may have a personal policy about always getting to a train station early or waiting until the last possible minute to submit reports and assignments or meet deadlines. They might talk about government policies, often in terms of how they do not seem to work. They almost certainly will talk about local policies in their workplace and how they have to follow through changes as a result of a new policy coming into force. If we are going to analyse policy, how it is made, how it is enacted and how effective it is, it is a good idea to try to define what we mean by the term 'policy'. Unfortunately, the word 'policy' has numerous definitions and means different things to different people in different contexts. Parsons (1995) has undertaken a systematic review of public policy and acknowledges the complexity of the field, but attempts to summarize it by drawing upon Heclo, who argues that policy is 'bigger than particular decisions but smaller than general social movements' (1972: 84) and that policy is more than an intended course of action. Recourse to the dictionary provides multiple definitions ranging from 'political sagacity' and 'craftiness' to 'a course of action adopted by government'. I like the idea that policy involves a course of action, and it need not be confined to government activity.

The next stage in discussing policy is to analyse how it comes into force and how it is implemented. There is a vast literature on the process of policymaking and this has come to be known as *policy analysis*. Even this area of academic scrutiny is not simple as there are a variety of theories that attempt to explain what occurs during policymaking, so much so that Parsons argues that policy analysis is essentially a 'boot-strapping activity' (1995: 73), and that no single theory or model is adequate to explain the complexity of the policy activity of the modern state.

The major focus of policymaking in education is part of the wider arena of public policy. Again, this needs some definition. Public policy is distinguished from the notion of that which is 'private', and analysis of the development of this area of policy stems from the early world of the Greeks who, through Aristotle, identified the tension between public and private spheres, particularly in terms of how much interference public policy can make in private spheres. Over time there has been a blurring of boundaries between public and private, so much so that today many 'problems' that were private in the past are considered to be in the public domain. In England the current frenetic activity of public policymaking stems from the increasing role of the state in trying to deal with numerous problems including those affecting housing, health and education. Education is a large component of *public* policy.

> 'Education has perhaps been the most complex and burdened of services. As the keystone of public policy-making and social reform in the postwar period, education has been expected to fuel economic growth, facilitate equality of opportunity and afford some social justice to the deprived: to educate has been to bring a new world out of the old. To accomplish this burdensome collective vision, education has had to manage the most complex network of relationships which cuts across communities, services, authorities and levels of government.' (Ranson 1985: 103)

This chapter attempts to discuss the main approaches to analysing policy, to help provide a framework within which particular education problems have been addressed in the past few years. Analysis of public policy involves the 'appreciation of the network of ideas, concepts and words which form the world of explanation within which policy-making and analysis takes place' (Parsons 1995: 73). It was Harold Lasswell who created the idea of the policy sciences (and the role of the policy analyst) in which knowledge *of* the policy process and knowledge *in* the policy process was examined (Lasswell 1970). Since then a veritable industry of policy analysis has been created. This is partly because the reaches of public policy are extensive and the complexity of the activity and its consequences continue to exercise the minds of policy analysts today. Policy analysts draw upon numerous 'frames' to help structure their study of public policy and these frames are not necessarily incommensurate or exclusive. Thus, one approach may focus on the social structure in which policy is made, whereas another may focus on management structures and systems. Furthermore, a philosophical framework might draw upon Rawls and Nozick's theories of justice or John Dewey's pragmatism. These frames can then be used to analyse particular issues, such as the impact of creating specialist colleges or of changing the national qualifications framework.

Rational policymaking

As there are many ways to analyse policy, I want to begin with describing the attempts made particularly since the middle of the last century to capture not only what policy is but what effect it has on the public. Early proponents of policy analysis argued that policy is essentially a rational process that attempts to solve problems (see Simon 1957). Any public issue, for example how to ensure young people achieve the necessary qualifications to be able to gain work, can be seen as a problem to be solved. A policy is simply a process by which the problem is defined, solutions identified and action taken. Lindblom (1959) identified policy as the science of 'muddling through' whereas Dror (1967) advocated an economically rational, scientific approach. Readers will immediately see that in the context of further education rationality is not necessarily the first characteristic of public policymaking! In fact, both Simon and Lindblom realized that bureaucracies are characterized by a great deal of irrationality, and Simon argued that most public policy involved decision-making that was characterized by 'bounded rationality', something that could be improved.

Lindblom's contribution to policy analysis took account of the incrementalism of public policymaking, and in his later years he argued that policy is not formed by a deliberate process at all but is a complex interactive process. He argued that any analysis of the policy process has to take account of a variety of what would now be called 'stakeholders', such as interest groups, plus the 'deeper forces' of inequality (Lindblom and Woodhouse 1993).

The assumption that policymaking is a rational, scientific process was also challenged by Etzioni (1968) and Hogwood and Gunn (1984), who argued that the rational model ignores the dimensions of power and legitimacy. Etzioni, in particular, has suggested that policy analysis should cover not only the 'problems' but also the policy options, or 'solutions' (Parsons 1995: 54). The helpful model of policy analysis, which views policy as problem-solving, proposes that we test the effectiveness of policy in its ability to solve problems, taking account of the unintended consequences of that policy. It is not easy to implement policy as there are always constraints in resources, both human and physical, and, of course, new policies are drafted onto existing policies that are still in force. This brings us to the notion that some problems and solutions have better chances of being dealt with than others, because of the existence of deeper factors in the policy arena, namely issues of power and legitimacy, as well as those of ideology. In other words, policy processes are politically highly charged and therefore may not be informed by rational argument or draw upon research evidence prior to their creation and implementation. Power in policy terms relates to how problems reach an agenda and influence decision-making to act although, as Parsons notes, 'real power in the policy process is the power to make non-decisions, that is the capacity of one group to prevent the ideas, concerns, interests and problems of another group getting "on" the agenda in the first place' (Parsons 1995: 86). Indeed, the most dangerous situation can be one in which no action is taken, as Pratt warns: 'Uninformed or ill-informed action is dangerous, but so too is inaction' (Pratt 1999: 40).

'Garbage can' approach

How do organizations take action? They may 'satisfice' rather than maximize solutions to problems. An interesting view of how they do this uses the metaphor of a garbage can (Cohen *et al.* 1972). These analysts argue that the way in which decisions are made about policy are almost serendipitous. Instead of policies that find solutions to problems, solutions exist and are 'in search of' problems. This view tries to explain how people in institutions dump various kinds of problems and solutions as they are generated, willy nilly, rather than rationally. In any single garbage can, there is a mix of solutions and problems, and of course, some cans are cleaned out more often than others. As Parsons notes:

> 'What the garbage can idea graphically suggests is that issues, problems and solutions are messy, untidy sorts of things, whose mode of identification by policy makers will depend on the time it was picked up, and the availability of cans to put them in.' (Parsons 1995: 302)

Stagist approaches

We need to consider how other influences, such as the way people think about problems and therefore how they identify solutions, interact with the creation and implementation of policy. One way to do this is to examine how policymaking moves forward through a series of short steps or sequences, often known as a 'stagist approach'. There are a number of writers who advocate the analysis of policy through examining how policy moves through cycles. Of all the ways to analyse policy, one of the most pervasive is to think of policy as a process and to try and map the stages and cycles it goes through. In this approach policy is seen as a simple cycle in which problems are defined, alternative responses and solutions are identified, options are evaluated, policy options are selected, then implemented and further evaluated.

The cyclical nature of policy can be examined:

- as it reaches the agenda
- as it becomes formulated and refined
- as a statement of problem definition

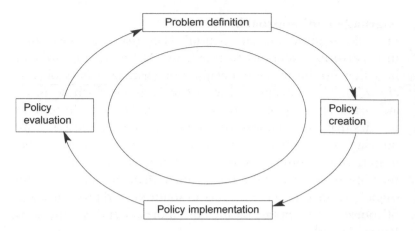

Figure 1 Policy cycle

- as it is implemented
- as it is changed
- as it leads to new policy formation.

Hogwood and Gunn (1984) suggest policymaking decisions are not necessarily rational and are influenced by a variety of forces. The cyclical nature of policymaking is not chronologically systematic and in no way takes account of all the deeper complexities of the use of power, agency and discourse, which continually shift and change the way in which any one issue is represented and the way in which people engage with, and challenge, the policies being created and implemented. Lasswell (1956) argued that the decision process involved the stages of intelligence, promotion, prescription, innovation, application, termination and appraisal. Hogwood and Gunn (1984) suggested that policy starts with agenda setting and moves through a series of stages including issue filtration and deciding on a particular solution, through to implementation and finally policy evaluation (Hogwood and Gunn 1984). Their analysis not only takes account of the stages that policy formation goes through but also identifies the complexities of any one stage, through weighting particular components. Thus, if an issue such as bullying in schools is seen to be fairly low-level, as an issue 'on the horizon', then it will not reach the agenda compared with truanting, if such an issue has suddenly become a 'hot topic' following media interest. The prioritizing of one issue to be dealt with over another begins to explain why policies follow fast and furious from the DfES, as certain topics become more publicized and the government is expected to take action.

The stagist approach has been criticized, partly because it provides a fairly artificial view of what happens in practice, and also because the real world is definitely less tidy and cyclical than the approach conveys. More importantly, the stagist approach does not help explain how policy moves from one stage to another, tends to focus on the 'top-down' aspects and therefore ignores the 'street-level' actors and misses the way in which, for example, evaluation does occur throughout a policy life, rather than just at the end. The policy world is not that tidy, yet at least this approach provides a framework within which to understand the dynamic and complex nature of policy. The stagist approach is a good heuristic device to help guide us through the complexities of policymaking.

System approaches
Policymaking is very amenable to metaphor and one way to describe it is to use the metaphor of networks, sub-systems and communities. In this depiction of policy, the process of policymaking is seen in terms of inputs, and outputs, and can in some ways be aligned with the idea that policymaking occurs in stages. Easton (1965) identified a political system model for policy analysis which was highly influential in contributing to the notion that policy receives inputs flowing from the environment, mediated through input channels such as interest groups and the media, along with demands from the political system, so that the conversion of these flows results in policy outputs and outcomes. It is easy to see that this model lends itself to the notion of target setting in which inputs and outputs can be quantified and performance measured. Later writers such as Almond et al. (1993) consider a model of a political system comprising: inputs, which are composed of interest articulation; process functions such as policymaking and policy implementation; and policy functions such as regulation and distribution. The policy output is fed back into a political system

which is part of a national and international environment. Institutions play a key role in this model as they mediate between government and people, particularly in the policy functions.

Pluralist–elitist approaches

A different approach emphasizes that policymaking involves the management of limited resources by people with differing levels of power and agency and that policy is implemented by other groups of people who also have differing levels of commitment and ability to act upon situations that are complex, dynamic and controversial. There are two main approaches within this paradigm: the work of the neo-Marxists (Gramsci 1994, Marcuse 1972); and that of those theorists broadly considered to be 'post-structuralist', such as Foucault (1970). Neo-Marxists, along with Hogwood and Gunn, examine policy through the ways in which some issues reach the decision-making phase and others are excluded from it. They do so by paying attention to the ideological or psychological processes in society that do not necessarily appear in the surface level of power. Relevant here is the notion of 'hegemony', in which certain groups dominate all aspects of civil society, and this domination is not explicit but is nevertheless pervasive. Thus people with 'social capital', such as middle-class people, know how to exploit the education system to gain qualifications and then professional jobs, which control public services and government (see Field 2000 and Schuller *et al.* 2004). Social capital is a concept that develops the notion of cultural capital used by Bourdieu, whereby certain groups in society enjoy advantages because they have developed certain 'sensitivities' and 'awareness' (see, for example, Bourdieu and Passeron 1977). Policy is concentrated in the hands of a few individuals or groups, with the powerless mass underneath, forming an 'iron triangle'. The elites who have power could include those who gain it through force (such as military elites) and those who gain it with propaganda skills (who have employed 'spin doctors'). The pluralist analysis is a normative one that argues for the involvement of different interest groups in policymaking, thus counterbalancing the dangers of concentrating decision-making power in the hands of elite groups.

Policy discourse approaches

Post-structuralists adopt the 'argumentative' approach, focusing on how language *shapes* the way in which we make sense of the world. Our language is not neutral, and therefore the way in which policymaking occurs is through a 'never ending series of communications and strategic moves by which various policy actors in loosely coupled forums of public deliberation construct intersubjective meanings' (Hoppe 1993: 77).

Policymaking and implementation can be examined in terms of their narrative and discourse. This approach, stemming primarily from critical theory and the work of Foucault (1970), Bourdieu (1977) and Habermas (1981), examines the way in which policies have been *framed*, rather than simply examining the stated aims and outcomes of policy.

Fischer and Forrester (1993) tried to raise awareness of the consequences of the role of language in policymaking when they argued that language 'doesn't just mirror reality; it actively shapes the way we perceive and understand it'.

> 'Worldviews are not made out of whole cloth but are shaped, incrementally and painfully, in the struggle of everyday people with concrete, ambiguous, tenacious, practical problems and questions ... their validity and feasibility are assessed in communities of people who are knowledgeable about the problem at hand, and who are all too conscious of the political, financial and practical constraints that define the situation for which they bear responsibility.' (Hajer and Wagenaar 2003: 14)

Deliberative policy analysis

A really good way to analyse policymaking is to move away from the idea that policy is the responsibility of one group of people such as politicians, to the acknowledgement that in today's networked society there are numerous individuals and groups who can, and possibly should, participate in the decision-making process. This approach looks at the idea of *governance*, rather than government.

This idea, advocated by writers such as Fischer and Forrester (1993) and Hajer and Wagenaar (2003), acknowledges the dissatisfaction with the limitations of 'set solutions' to difficult political issues which have tended to be imposed by government intervention in a top-down way. Using the word 'governance' opens up a new way of thinking about governing and political decision-making. In particular, Hajer and Wagenaar argue that the language of 'governance' can help practitioners and theorists to 'break out of tacit patterns of thinking' (2003: 2). A corollary of this is that more people can become involved in the decision-making process, and this leads to a more open-ended way to approach dealing with the problems that are largely intractable, or 'wicked' (Lo Bianco and Freebody 1997). If people can become involved in helping create policies that will affect them personally, they may help create different solutions, informed by their personal knowledge of what has happened to them when previous policies were enacted.

Using lenses
A different way to approach policy analysis is to examine the decision-making that occurs as part of the process of policy formation. One way to do this is to use the idea of 'lenses', in which any particular event can be interpreted by taking different views of the one phenomenon. Allison (1971) used this approach to examine a very complex event, the Cuban missile crisis, and argued that three lenses could be used: one that looked at the 'rational actor', i.e. government decision-making; one that looked at the organizational process, such as the involvement of the actual organizations comprising national government; and finally one that looked at the bureaucratic politics, such as the players and their interests. Although this approach has been criticized because it can over-simplify a complex situation, I like it, as it allows for contentious perspectives to co-exist, rather than attempting to describe a once and for all 'reality'.

Perhaps, as Parsons argues, the main point about policy analysis is that any orientation towards public policy and the problems being addressed by policy do not exist in 'neat, tidy, academic boxes' (Parsons 1995: 64). We can use metaphors and models to help us explain what we see (and make us aware of what we might not be able to see). However, we must be aware that any of these frames are heuristics that have limitations, and it may be more helpful to utilize multiple frames and lenses, providing we remember that we are imposing stages, cycles or values on complex events which are incredibly interactive and fluid.

We need to think about what policy analysis is *for*. Is it to help us understand how a particular policy was created and enacted and to ascertain the consequences? Is it to seek ways to deal more effectively with the problem or issue that the policy was attempting to address? Or is it to find ways to make policy more effectively? These are very different reasons and the first question addresses the *how* rather than the *what for* of policy-making. I suspect that many analyses of policymaking are less clear about this, with some confusion about 'how to make an issue better' rather than 'how to make the policymaking process better', or 'what the policy is for in the first place'. As Pratt argues (1999), there is an idealism about some of the main policy analysis approaches, with Simon (1957), Lindblom (1959) and Dror (1967) arguing for the ideal, albeit unattainable, goal of rationality. Pratt suggests that a more appropriate alternative is the realist approach, which 'allows' multiple formulations of the problem that can subsequently be tested. The analysis focuses on the outcomes of any policy method, but the realist approach starts by treating policy as a hypothesis which can be tested through conducting an experiment, along the lines of 'if we do this, then that outcome should follow'. The effectiveness of the policy is then established by examining the results of the 'experiment'. To argue his case, Pratt draws on the work of Karl Popper, who developed the notion of *falsification* to help examine how our knowledge about the world develops. Popper argued that we cannot establish the truth about anything, but we can establish when any of our premises is false, and this is a fruitful means of developing our knowledge of the world. In other words, we are more likely to learn something when it doesn't work than when it does. In policy terms we look for the unintended consequences of policies as well as the intended consequences and we search out whether or not the aims of policy have been met, not in the sense of 'if we do this, x will happen' but 'when we did do this, y happened instead'.

This approach to policymaking, too, takes a different perspective, in which the problem has to be defined, and when the solution is 'found' it is treated as an experiment, rather than as an assumption that the solution will successfully address the problem. The helpful aspect of this approach, then, is that policies are not seen so much as failures but as experiments that did not work. This allows us to try alternative solutions and also ensures that we have more knowledge about the issue at hand; or at least about how *not* to deal with it!

Criticisms of any policy analysis approach

Any policy analysis approach and framework is only as good as the perspective it represents. We need to remember the distinction between policy analysis reflecting what *is* as opposed to what *ought to be*. Thus, criticisms of a policy failure may relate to what happened to the solution that was attempting to address a problem or issue, but they may also relate to the type of policy solution adopted and therefore not refer to the consequences of the policy but the way in which the policy was used.

Hajer and Wagenaar (2003) pinpoint a possible reason for the fact that policy *analysis* does not always help move policy*making* forward. This is because they consider that analysis of social problems 'is at heart a cerebral, armchair activity' (page 19). One of the reasons for the ineffectiveness and irrelevance of policy analysis as theoretical rationality of the policy sciences is a Cartesian bias which results in a gap between the theoretical rationality of the policy sciences and the practical rationality of the practitioner. People making policy, and those administering it, are obliged to find solutions for concrete, specific issues in those areas for which they are responsible. However, the actions that policymakers and administrators carry out involve practical judgement, reflection, knowledge and experience. The reality is that:

> 'We see practitioners of very different plumage wrestle with conflict, power, uncertainty and unpredictability. Solutions are not so much formulated as arrived at, haltingly, tentatively, through acting upon the situation at hand and through

the application of practical wisdom in negotiating concrete situations ... consequently, the role of policy analysis changes too. It is not longer about the invention of solutions for society; it often finds itself in the "mud" of policy practice, trying to assist in the discovery of new policy options and the formulation of compelling arguments ... Traditional policy science focuses on "problems" and "decisions". We suggest that a reformulated, deliberative policy science takes practices as its unit of analysis.' (Hajer and Wagenaar 2003: 19)

Policy analysis in practice

Many readers will be only too aware of the gap between policy creation and successful implementation, or the 'implementation gap' (Barrett and Fudge 1981: 251). Regardless of the policy analysis approach employed, fundamental questions about how policies come into being and how they are implemented have to consider the original policy aims and what actually happened. Implicit in the analysis is the idea that if a policy works, certain things should have happened and, conversely, if the policy hasn't worked, certain things that should have happened have not done so. There is a normative underpinning for nearly any policy analysis as the framework applied contains inherent values. For example, a discourse analysis of the introduction of the national curriculum for adult basic skills will seek out the silences as well as the ways in which words are used to define certain problems. There is an expectation that certain forms of discourse are more acceptable than others because even the words used in discourse analysis are value-laden, for example the term 'permissive' to describe how a particular phrasing in a document allows rather than constrains subsequent action. In a systems approach, the sub-systems that 'should' be in place are those that are analysed, to look for blockages, under efficiency and malfunction. It is difficult to apply a neutral, objective analysis to any form of human endeavour as people are influenced by their culture, their position in society and their views about how to go about solving problems but it is important to recognize this when analysing what happened when any policy has been implemented. This is something easily forgotten when one is the subject of that policy or is being expected to change practice, to conform or to comply with a new policy.

The two basic ways to implement policy are through compliant or performative routes, probably better understood as 'stick and carrot' approaches. Barrett and Fudge (1981) argue that if the assumption behind successful policy implementation is that control or compliance can be achieved by putting the right incentives or sanctions in place, then any compromise in the process of policy implementation will be seen by the policymakers as a policy failure. On the other hand, if policy implementation is about 'getting something done' then the emphasis moves from compliance to performance and consequently the analysis of that policy's effectiveness changes. Of course this assumes that the original policy has clear intentions and is accepted by all those concerned with its implementation. Ambiguity in policy intent often arises because of a multiplicity of goals or intentions, some of which may be in conflict with one another:

> 'If policy is formulated, modified and translated into frameworks for action in a series of negotiative processes between groups of actors and agencies, it is hardly surprising that the resultant compromises produce "policy" that is less than coherent and may appear to have several conflicting objectives.' (Barrett and Fudge 1981: 274)

Observation of what happens in practice shows that certain individuals, groups or governments tend to find a way of doing, or getting done, what they *really want to do* while others do not (Barrett and Fudge 1981: 275, original italics). For example, some individuals believe that 'the end justifies the means' and in more extreme cases some people will stop at nothing to achieve their own intentions. It is easy to imagine how tension arises where there are differences of opinion about how to achieve a particular goal. There are, too, ethical considerations about whether the end can justify the means.

The deliberative policy analysis (DPA) approach

As noted above, if, instead of looking at a policy in terms of what it sets out to do, and how it got to be there in the first place, we look at the practices that any policy affects, then our lens shifts to looking at the people involved, and what they actually do. Hajer and Wagenaar (2003) propose a deliberative policy analysis (DPA), which acknowledges that people have a multitude of perspectives and, indeed, if we look at how any issue is defined (as Pratt (1999) would argue that we should), then immediately we can see that people will dispute how an issue is defined. This will account for the ways in which people subvert policy aims or even deny that a policy is necessary. Thus arguments over whether people should demonstrate their learning through gaining qualifications depends on what people think that qualifications are for. Are they able to test learning or provide a proxy for learning, are they used in the workplace as signals to allow people with qualifications into certain levels of responsibility with accompanying levels of remuneration? Each of these views will direct a different response to a policy which introduces a requirement that all learners in further education must gain (or at least work towards) a qualification on any funded programme by the Learning and Skills Council (LSC). What does this mean, then, for college managers who are responsible for running a range of programmes and must decide which will be viable, measuring this through the use of performance indicators including achievement of qualifications? Managers are involved in making practical judgements, which are:

> 'immediate, intuitive, concrete, interactive, pragmatic, personal and action-oriented. Moreover, practical judgement is something that comes naturally to people. It is something they do in the course of their everyday activities, usually without giving it much thought.' (Hajer and Wagenaar 2003: 22)

The trouble is, most of these practical judgements have to work within a variety of constraints. In the example above, there may be programmes that do not meet the criteria of viability in funding terms but without which learners cannot progress to other more advanced programmes that are an important part of the college's portfolio. There may be competing programmes at similar level, possibly run in different departments. Given the multitude of constraints in most policy situations, practitioners cannot aspire to resolution of these conflicts, but they can try to discover a workable definition of the problem, or 'the temporary stabilization of a situation that is unhinged or threatens to become so, or the emergence of personal insight that allows the actor to function more effectively in the situation at hand' (Hajer and Wagenaar 2003: 23).

In other words, practitioners have to work with compromises but they have particular social identities that validate what they do and say, both to themselves and to the world at large. This is something that Bourdieu (1977, 1993) would describe as 'habitus'. The way in which people operate is subject to what is expected and permitted in their roles and in their environments. So, for example, managers are highly unlikely to ignore any qualifications system and instruct their lecturers to teach what they like. They work within a system and their language and practice helps define what this system is. Their language and practice also tends to make them so deeply embedded in this system that most of the time they will not even be aware that their perspectives are shaped by it.

Just as people have their own 'take' on a situation, they are also 'wedded' to their own way of construing it or framing it. Frames are highly resistant to change, being rooted in action. They seem to be so natural that they almost defy critical self-analysis. When people clash over conflicting understandings of a complex situation, a frame provides certainty. Such framings become institutionalized in practices. The way to attempt to do things differently in the teeth of conflict or policy failure becomes possible by developing 'constructive' doubt, which can help 'reframe the situation', perhaps by finding resonances with arguments and views available in the other public services outside education.

Critically reflective approaches to FE policy

The DPA approach to policy analysis encompasses a critically reflective approach, along similar lines to those taken by advocators of professional learning, for example Schon (1983, 1987), Brookfield (1995), Hillier (2002, 2005). In this approach we are asked to consider the 'taken for granted' practices that we execute and challenge them, or at least 'problematize' them. In policy terms, we need to ask naive questions such as 'how will this policy help our learners?' or 'why are we assuming that this is the way to do so?'. We need to ask who will be helped, who will be damaged and who will be ignored if a particular policy is implemented. We need to ask why this policy has come into being now and who was responsible for getting it enough prominence to become a policy. We also need to understand the role we play in executing policy, and our reactions to it, including the potential choice of deciding to do nothing.

Hillier and Jameson argued that FE institutional reactions to education policy could be typified through four kinds of responses: resistant, accommodatory, over-compliant and reflexive (2003: 29–33). Of course, these are not exclusive categories. Outright rejection of a policy, particularly if its provenance is from government, via the LSC, which involves large amounts of funding, is a highly unlikely response! Over-compliance, too, is less likely, except that some parts of an institution may follow certain rules slavishly while other parts are more accommodatory. For example, conducting teaching observations or making use of management information out-puts may be rigorously applied in one department and almost ignored in another unless an inspection is looming! People who accommodate new policies tend to water down their imple-mentation and there is a certain amount of reluctance to take new policies on board. This partly explains why some policies, once implemented, fail fully to meet their original objectives and why the outcomes may be very different from those intended. The process has to be managed through negotiation and as a result is likely to succeed, but the 'normative' nature of this response does not fully engage with the complexities of critically reflecting on something that may have to be imple-mented, even if it is likely to be quite damaging to the people it targets. Hillier and Jameson argue that the key point is for practitioners to engage with policy as we have some power to shape and adjust policy to fit our situations more closely.

'Instead of blindly rejecting or wholesale accepting new policy, instead of watering down initiatives defensively or reluctantly to accommodate policy change in only minor ways, we can both *enthusiastically* and *critically* evaluate new initiatives.' (Hillier and Jameson 2003: 32, original italics)

This approach accords with Ozga's definition of policy, which is 'struggled over, not delivered in tablets of stone, to a grateful or quiescent population' (2000: 1).

Ozga's argument attempts to help people who are involved in education to be able to contest policy in an informed way, through developing capacities that allow them to 'speak with authority against misguided, mistaken and unjust education policy' (page 1). Such speech is the result of researching education policy, not from the perspective of examining it on its pedestal, but from including a wide range of people in the inquiry, much in the same way as Hajer and Wagenaar (2003) advocate. The message is clear. If we are to engage critically with policy, its processes, its implementation and its impact, as well as evaluating how successful it is and what consequences result, then we need to understand what policy is, what it does, and what *we can do* to influence policy throughout its complex, dynamic life.

For managers in FE, then, there is an important job to do. Each policy that comes down from government or its agencies, such as the LSC, needs to be examined carefully, drawing upon the range of approaches outlined above. Understanding how policy can be monitored and evaluated throughout its 'cycle' will help ensure that damaging unintended consequences can be spotted early on, helping to lessen further impact. Being aware of the ways in which policy is talked about, i.e. its discourse, further empowers those who are the unwilling recipients of its focus. Managers are also aware that there has to be implementation of a variety of policies, at national, regional and local level. These are like spinning plates subject to a variety of forces, and therefore likely to come crashing down if not kept moving.

In the following chapters I have chosen some of the major components of further education activity to examine how policy has been developed and enacted. I have identified some of the consequences of these policies, where they are aligned and where they pull against each other. By the time you read this chapter, most current policies will be out of date, superseded by new pressing government and agency initiatives. I hope, though, that you will be able to engage with your critical reflection of, and your role in challenging, implementing and evaluating such policies, so that you can speak with authority and manage in an informed manner.

2 A recent history of post-compulsory policy from 1944

'The history of post-16 education and training in England and Wales since the end of the Second World War is one of makeshift and invariably short-lived initiatives and missed opportunities.' (Chitty 2000: 23)

Further education exists today because of certain government legislation in the past. As I argued in Chapter 1, some policies cannot be seen in isolation from other wider issues, and the way in which people have been offered technical and vocational education has been affected by the larger social problems that government has grappled with. Throughout the whole period under examination, though, there has been a constant urge to ensure that the working population has the necessary knowledge and skill to compete with other countries and to be at the forefront of technological development. Even though the current government agenda for skills is full of exhortation, a cursory glance as far back as the Forster Report in 1870 shows that the government has always been concerned that other countries have the competitive edge and that if we don't improve our own skills in the workforce, we are doomed to economic failure.

'Many of our labourers are utterly uneducated, are, for the most part, unskilled labourers and if we leave our work-folk any longer unskilled ... they will become overmatched in the competition of the world.' (in Fieldhouse 1996: 3)

A 'pre-history' of further education

There are defining moments in the history of further education that have been particularly influenced by government policy. The history of further education, though, stems from a rich and varied tapestry of action woven by government, local communities, business and industry groups and individual campaigners over the last two centuries in England. The rise of technical education was the precursor to the current further education context. Early in the nineteenth century, when England was undergoing massive changes in society due to the Industrial Revolution, the mechanics' institutes were established (from 1810). These institutes acted as mutual improvement societies and aimed to instruct their members in various branches of science and 'useful knowledge' (Kelly 1970: 121). Alternative movements such as the London Working Men's Association developed simultaneously, again aiming to help working-class people acquire knowledge of the arts and sciences. These movements were primarily philanthropic and voluntarist. It was not until the 1870 Education Act that schooling became compulsory, enabling children to grow into adulthood literate, numerate and employable. Technical education became enhanced by the establishment of the City and Guilds of London Institute in 1879, and the existing Society of Arts in 1882 turned its concentration to commercial subjects. The government was so concerned about the poor showing of British exhibits at the Paris Exhibition in 1887 that a select committee and two royal commissions were created to look at technical issues. The Technical Instruction Act of 1889 gave county and borough councils power to establish Technical Instruction Committees and to devote a penny per person from the rates to 'technical and manual' instruction. Readers will be interested to know that these ventures were supported by funds gained from taxing alcoholic spirits. This 'whisky money' ensured that technical education was well established by the turn of the twentieth century, contributing nearly 90 per cent of public expenditure for this purpose.

The development of technical education began in earnest during the twentieth century. In 1938 there were 1.2 million students of technical and commercial education (Pratt 2000). A factor in this growth was the creation of a national system of examinations, the National Certificate Scheme. However, much of the provision was ad hoc and the government preferred voluntary initiatives to state intervention, particularly for technical education and adult education, which was seen as a low priority by comparison with compulsory schooling (Lucas 2000: 148). Indeed, the low status of this provision has continued to haunt those who argue for the value of adult continuing education today.

A sector becomes institutionalized

By 1944, the government realized that it needed to ensure all children had access to education until they were at least 15. The 1944 Education Act not only created a tripartite system in secondary education, with grammar, secondary modern and technical schools, it also established that local education authorities had responsibility for adults, too. The adult and further education systems were almost totally separate at this point, with adult education providing mainly 'liberal' education and further education providing technical and vocational education.

In 1959, the Crowther Report suggested that further education would be the next 'battleground of English education'. At the time many young people left school at 15 with few or no qualifications and either took up apprenticeships or simply went to work. Most of the young people the Crowther Report discussed have now reached retirement age, but adults in the workforce still constitute one part of the current government's target groups for the achievement of level 2 qualifications.

The primary pattern of provision in FE during this period was of day release programmes for young working men who were being trained 'off the job', with some full-time provision. The 1964 Industrial Training Act (ITA) had profound effects on vocational education and training. Although heavily criticized by employers for being intrusive and costly (Field 1996: 342), the ITA helped affirm the role of further education in providing the training required by apprentices. At the same time, some school leavers were opting for college provision rather than sixth forms and the FE sector began to earn its name as providing 'second chance' education (Green 1986: 100). As each local education authority (LEA) was responsible for provision, there were wide variations in the type and amount of technical education available. The geographical circumstances of some authorities required a focus on, for example, heavy engineering. Wider afield, government urged the development of technical education at higher levels through the Robbins Report in 1963, which established polytechnics to work alongside but differently from universities to ensure people gained the necessary high levels of knowledge required for vocational qualifications. These polytechnics and colleges of higher education, along with some specialist colleges, were responsible for providing courses leading to advanced further education, defined as being anything above A level, such as Higher National Diplomas (HNDs). The role of further education, then, was to act as the next tier down, continuing its role of providing technical and further education, known as 'non-advanced further education' or NAFE (Cantor *et al.* 1995). In addition, FE provided a broad range of programmes for adults and also some specialist provision, such as art and design or horticulture.

The 1970s

During the recession of the 1970s colleges experienced the need to transform themselves into institutions offering other more varied and general forms of provision. Thus, the technical nature of further education changed during this time to include general, further and multi-purpose education. Importantly for policy analysis, it was during the 1970s that government began to take a keen interest in education, primarily following the Ruskin speech (1976) by the then Labour Prime Minister, Jim Callaghan. By now, the country had undergone its first major recession as a result of the 1973 oil crisis and unemployment among young people and adults rose to 1.7 million. Any desire to train people employers may have had was now severely constrained by economic imperatives. Large numbers of people found themselves unqualified for jobs that were available, while those in work were frequently untrained and often unskilled. Yet many people did not want to work in industry even if they were qualified:

'I am concerned on my journeys to find complaints from industry that new recruits from schools sometimes do not have the necessary basic tools to do the job that is required. I have been concerned to find that many of our best trained students who have completed the higher levels of education at university or polytechnic have no desire or intention of joining industry ... there is no virtue in producing socially well adjusted members of society who are unemployed because they do not have the skills.' (Callaghan, Ruskin speech, 1976, quoted in Fawbert 2003: 316)

Demands that schools should cover vocational subjects were lessened by the knowledge that FE was a 'natural' site for helping young people move from school to work. Green (1986: 101) argues that it is also because FE was 'entrepreneurial' that it was a 'fertile soil for implanting ideas in education that are based on a market philosophy', something the Conservative government of the late 1970s and 1980s exploited.

The pattern of provision began to change during the 1970s. In some LEAs, tertiary colleges were established, which, like general further education colleges, provided education for 16–18-year-olds in their area (Devon LEA was the first to establish these in 1970). Sixth-form colleges, too, were created, providing full-time education, mainly A level courses for young people moving on from comprehensive schools that did not possess a sixth form. The structure of FE, then, was bound by policies affecting the compulsory education sector, particularly the moves to create comprehensive education, which aimed to draw together the separate grammar, secondary modern and the fast-disappearing technical schools.

Cantor *et al.* (1995) argue that it was during the 1970s and onwards that government felt it necessary to intervene directly in education and training policy to grapple with Britain's relatively poor record on skills training and that this intervention focused more on training than education. By now, further education was becoming a new 'tertiary' education system and was seen by Green as a political solution to economic and social problems caused by rising unemployment. The clearest example is the way in which FE developed a training paradigm to assimilate the Manpower Services Commission (MSC), created in 1974, with cross-party support, by the then Conservative government and which was initially responsible for planning jobs for the future. The MSC was meant to act as a single agency drawing together the activities of Industrial Training Boards (ITBs). Programmes began to come on stream with the creation of the Training Opportunities Scheme (TOPS) in 1973.

The 1980s

During the 1980s, mass youth unemployment featured heavily in government policymaking and further education found itself centrally involved in delivering programmes for young people and unemployed adults, including the Youth Opportunities Scheme (YOPS), shortly afterwards replaced by the Youth Training Scheme (YTS) and the Employment Training (ET) of the 1980s. Vehement criticism of what the MSC actually achieved is documented by Benn and Fairly (1986), who show how during the rise of rapid unemployment, rather than creating jobs, the MSC oversaw the destruction of skills centres and ITBs and a drastic decrease in apprenticeships.

In 1981, the government published a White Paper, *A New Training Initiative: Programme for Action*, which set out a pro-gramme for improving training, including the creation of industry standards to replace the age-restricted, time-serving style of apprenticeship training. The idea behind the White Paper was to try and specify outcomes that would be obtained from vocational qualifications. A further White Paper, *Working Together: Education and Training* (1986) reinforced the govern-ment's aim to establish standards of competence. There were two government ministries behind the White Paper, the then Department of Education and Science (DES) and the Employment Department (ED). One of the recommendations was to establish a National Council for Vocational Qualifica-tions (NCVQ), which was set up later that year. By 1989, a further White Paper, *Employment for the 1990s*, argued that it was necessary to develop a strategy of 'training through life' to enable Britain to 'continue to grow and generate jobs'. The paper argued that the 'prime responsibility for this investment lies with employers'.

While the government was focusing on the creation of industry standards and a vocational qualifications system that would be competence-based (of which more in Chapter 5), those in the FE sector were finding themselves being required to change fundamentally the way in which they taught vocational programmes. A different kind of vocational education and training was being proselytized and the focus on training for skills was seen by FE tutors as omitting the essential learning that fosters understanding.

The rise of new vocationalism affected the role of FE, in which people were now being prepared *for* work rather than having their skills updated *in* work (Bloomer 1997: 14). Such preparation took on the idea that learners needed to develop skills such as the ability to collaborate with work colleagues, and also that they needed to be prepared for 'life'. Even the curriculum reflected this change, with 'life skills' being an important component of government-funded unemployment programmes such as TOPS, YOPS and YTS.

Comparisons with Europe began to drive government policymaking on a number of fronts that affected further education. Staying-on rates of young people in full-time education were very poor compared with their European counterparts. In 1987, only 50 per cent of 16-year-olds were participating in full-time education compared with, for example, 91 per cent in Sweden. The figure was much worse for 16–18-year-olds, with only 35 per cent in the UK compared with 76 per cent in Sweden (Finegold 1993: 41).

Employers prepared to fund training were also seen to be sadly lacking by comparison with their European counterparts. Furthermore, the system in England had produced a 'low-skills' economy, in which the majority of enterprises had poorly trained managers and workers producing low-quality goods and services (Finegold and Soskice 1988). One of the primary challenges, then, in 'upskilling' the workforce was not only to encourage people to enter the workforce fully qualified but also to ensure employers took responsibility for training their employees, all within a standardized system in which outputs such as competences could be easily measured. These strategies are partially responsible for the rise in the use of performance indicators and an accountability framework.

A different kind of government legislation fundamentally altered the management and governance of FE in 1988. The Education Reform Act (ERA) stripped LEAs of their control of colleges and financial responsibility was delegated to FE colleges with more than 200 full-time-equivalent enrolments. The government bodies were reconstituted and more than half their members had to be drawn from industry or be independent of the local authority and college.

So by the end of the 1980s, FE was being required to adapt to a different qualifications system based on industry standards and competences, to be responsible for its own management and to liaise with local Training and Enterprise Councils (TECs) over workforce development. It was clear, then, that the policies affecting the sector were drawing in control, on the one hand, through regulating management and governance and, on the other, by defining the type of training and qualifications that the sector should provide.

The 1990s

> 'The education and training system in England is notoriously fragmented and, being an "extended" policy community, is subject to the competing demands of multiple interest groups. The 16–19 debate illustrates this fully and in under two years (July 1989–May 1991) 52 separate sets of recommendations for 16–19 reform occurred.' (Richardson et al. 1993: 13)

If the 1980s were characterized by vocationalism and credentialism, the 1990s became the decade that represented a major shift in government policy towards the FE education and training sector, characterized by an 'open market' policy with increasing accountability and interference. In 1991, the government produced a White Paper entitled *Education and Training for the 21st Century*, which was written by the DES and the ED. It proposed to end the 'artificial divide' between academic and vocational qualifications for young people, to promote the engagement of employers through the TECs and to give colleges freedom to expand their provision. The way to achieve this was to separate colleges from any involvement with their LEAs and to establish a single body that would fund the provision. The White Paper led to the 1992 Further and Higher Education (FHE) Act. A new funding council, the Further Education Funding Council (FEFC), was set up, responsible to the Secretary of State for Education. Under the Act, 465 colleges became self-governing, as corporate bodies with powers to employ their own staff and manage their own assets and resources. Governing bodies were required to have a member of the local TEC but, interestingly, no one from the LEA, reinforcing the notion that employers must be part of the governance of the institution and that LEAs must now relinquish their powers.

The comparative freedom granted to colleges to manage their own affairs led to a frenzy of activity. Colleges recruited business managers responsible for introducing management information systems. They appointed entrepreneurial managers who were willing to go and 'win' business through franchise arrangements and by wooing employers prepared to fund training for their employees. Other government legislation, including European legislation, for example on health and safety, ensured a steady stream of business to the colleges. Colleges competed with school sixth forms and tertiary colleges for students and the competitive era of FE management was born. There was cut-throat competition in setting fees, in creating attractive packages to woo students from one institution to another and in the range of the curriculum on offer. This expanded to take advantage of the funding mechanism, so that, providing any programme met the criteria for funding through the Schedule 2 of the 1992 FHE Act, any college could 'sell' any learning opportunity to anybody! As there had been a demand-led element to the funding system, initially with no cap, colleges could earn a standard fee for every student recruited beyond their target agreed with the FEFC. As Smithers and Robinson note,

'The unprecedented energy that was released might have been containable had a secure qualifications structure been in place but the newly emerging colleges were hit by the double whammy of a new funding methodology and a novel approach to qualifying people.' (Smithers and Robinson 2000: 7)

By 1998, the FEFC surveyed franchise provision ('collaborative provision') and discovered that it had grown from 5 per cent in 1994 to 19 per cent in 1997 and that over 58 per cent was concentrated in just 20 colleges (some of these notoriously encountered financial difficulties, were investigated for their financial affairs and were even closed down, for example Bilston College in 1995 and Halton College in 1999).

The government appeared to be running two contradictory reform strategies through the incorporation of further education: the funding system for colleges, which rewarded them for recruiting more students; and the TECs' funding system, operated by an output-related funding mechanism that was locally driven. These two contrasting systems are seen by Finegold (1993) as a product of:

'a major weakness in the policy-making structure – the absence of coordination of education, training and labour market policy either within or between departments. Britain stands alone among the main European nations for its failure to establish a well-financed, independent organization that is able to develop and evaluate policy in this rapidly changing field.' (Finegold 1993: 52)

Some of the policy aims of the previous decade, particularly those aimed at increasing the number of young people staying on beyond the minimum leaving age, were achieved during the 1990s. By 1993, 70 per cent of 16-year-olds were staying in full-time education after the minimum leaving age. The colleges were enormously successful in recruiting additional students and their average unit of funding was driven downwards as numbers of students were driven upwards.

As noted in Chapter 1, there are always unintended consequences arising from any policy. In the FE sector, as colleges were squeezed financially through competition and the funding mechanism, the impact was felt particularly by staff. Staff were employed on new contracts, replacing the 'Silver Book' conditions, which had initially been created to attract people skilled in crafts to enter lecturing. By 1995–6, 55 per cent of all staffing FE were working part-time (Taubman 2000). They became disenfranchized by the creation of employment agencies and lost employment rights. The casualization of the sector (Betts 2000; Hillier and Jameson 2004) has continued to have profound implications for the management of staff in the sector and for the achievement of quality, though it must be emphasized that part-time staff are usually highly professional in their approach to teaching but may not always have the necessary institutional support and facilities required to meet quality standards.

For managers in further education, the incorporation of the colleges in April 1993 was perhaps the most profound change that they would have to deal with in the entire history of further education. They had to manage a complex funding system, with tariffs and weightings, programmes deconstructed into guided learning hours and the identification of recruitment, retention and achievement rates. They also had to try and maximize funding, primarily through the recruitment of as many students as possible: a strategy known throughout the sector as getting 'bums on seats'.

From competition to collaboration

Anyone who was involved in managing further education in the late 1990s will be familiar with the sudden rush of reports, Green and White Papers that characterized the change of government in 1997. When New Labour was elected, it was on the manifesto of 'education, education, education'. College principals throughout the country looked forward to a recognition of the role that FE played in helping young people and adults gain knowledge, skills and qualifications. By the time New Labour came to power, FE had become a diversified sector, working across a range of partnerships with TECs, employers, voluntary organizations, adult and community partnerships, higher education institutes and schools. Young people who were not succeeding in their secondary schools were beginning to be welcomed into small pockets of provision in the colleges. The boundaries between further education and every other form of formal learning provision in the country were blurring.

The major policies emanating from the New Labour government took account of the need for lifelong learning. Again, this was not an initiative peculiar to England but stemming from European deliberations on education and training, notably the White Paper in 1995. This was followed by the European Union *Memorandum on Lifelong Learning* (2000). The Organization for Economic Cooperation and Development (OECD) had begun to publish more analyses of education and training in its member countries and comparisons between countries began to be formalized through international surveys, such as the international adult literacy survey (IALS) and the programme of international student assessment (PISA).

Back in England, Helena Kennedy produced a report addressing the question 'what is FE for?' Her report, *Learning Works* (1997), became seminal as a battle cry for those in FE to continue its good work on widening participation, particularly for those who had not done well at school: as Kennedy noted, 'if at first you don't succeed, you don't succeed' (p. 21). At the same time, the government had created an advisory group, chaired by Sir Robert Fryer, to examine lifelong learning, and its first report was published at the end of 1997 (NAGCELL 1997).

The Kennedy report was followed swiftly by the government's Green Paper (downgraded from the original intention to publish a White Paper) called *The Learning Age* (DfEE 1998), which argued that there needed to be a tripartite partnership between providers, employers and individuals. The government wanted to create a new way for adults to learn, taking advantage of technology, through the creation initially of the University for Industry (UfI) and its operational arm, learndirect, with funding for adults through the use of individual learning accounts (which became subject to fraudulent misuse by some training organizations and were subsequently withdrawn).

After *The Learning Age*, the government produced its next White Paper, *Learning to Succeed* (DfEE 1999), which set out the framework for the way in which the sector would be structured to meet the challenges laid down in *The Learning Age*. Now the government identified a need to draw together the disparate agencies involved in post-compulsory education and training. Instead of separate bodies, the TEC and FEFC, a new body, the Learning and Skills Council (LSC), would be created, which would fund all post-compulsory education with the exception of higher education. Both *The Learning Age* and *Learning to Succeed* argued that further education is vital for forging an inclusive society and that the sector can play a major economic role in raising the country's economic strength and morale: so much so that 'if you are not in a school sixth form, at work or at a university, then you should be involved with the local college' (Lucas 2000: 153).

At the same time that the overarching policy framework was being set by the government White Papers, specific areas of lifelong learning were being targeted. 1n 1999, Claus Moser reported on the state of adult basic skills in his report *A Fresh Start: Improving Literacy and Numeracy* (DfEE 1999), which led to the Skills for Life strategy of 2000, discussed in more detail in Chapter 4.

2000 – another decade, another change

By the beginning of the new millennium, further education was about to go through another restructuring. The colleges, of course, continued, but their funding and overall management was about to change again. During 2000–6 there has been a plethora of activity by government, which can only be described as one of increasing control, but one which addressed the two major aims of: (i) creating an inclusive society which is (ii) also economically successful. The following chapters address these current policies and how they have affected, and continue to affect, the role of FE today.

Hodgson and Spours identify six strands to government policy from the late 1990s, which I will examine here in relation to the further education sector. The first strand is what they call the 'adult learning opportunities strand' and is diffused through *The Learning Age* (1998), the reports of the National Advisory Group for Continuing Education and Lifelong Learning (NAGCELL 1997, 1999) and the Moser Report (1999). All these reports advocated motivating learners to participate in education and training opportunities through the use of strategies to stimulate demand, improve the learning environment and provide incentives.

The second strand is 'social exclusion'. The government set up initiatives such as the New Deal programme for both young people and (subsequently) older learners, to help them become involved in the workplace by widening the range of learning opportunities available. This policy strand links with other government policies, such as on welfare and housing, arising from collaboration between government departments. The underlying aim for such collaboration is to target specific learner groups, particularly marginalized and excluded groups, more effectively. These two strands run through the following chapters but are particularly noticeable in Chapters 3 and 4.

Third, the government has worked on policies aimed at qualifications reform. This strand has a long history of strategy, planning and reform, although as I write today, there is still no resolution to the problem of finding ways to create a simple, inclusive framework that will operate effectively for all learners, whatever their age, and which is meaningful to individuals, parents, employers and education and training providers. Chapter 5 outlines the major features of this policy strand.

A fourth strand is aimed at skills and work-based learning and can be seen in government reports such as the *National Skills Task Force: Towards a National Skills Agenda* (DfEE 1999), *Tackling the Adult Skills Gap* (DfEE 2000) and more recently *Realising our Potential* (DfES 2003) and *Skills: Getting on in Business, Getting on at Work* (DfES 2006). This strand can be seen across the other strands, particularly in relation to qualifications and in relation to the Success for All strategy, with its targets and strategies, outlined in Chapter 3.

The fifth strand addresses the funding and organization of post-16 learning, but it has increasingly changed its boundaries to include 14–16-year-olds. The government's White Paper

(2005) is an example of this. Such policies are not universally welcome, as Lumby and Foskett argue:

'[the] rising wave of anxiety that education and training do not do right by our young people, and that the implications are (and will be) widely felt in our society has finally crashed on the policy shore.' (Lumby and Foskett 2005: vii)

This strand is linked to the reorganization of the learning and skills sector and is discussed in Chapter 3.

Finally, there is government policymaking aimed at quality. This, again, is an area that permeates (implicitly and usually explicitly) all other policies. Chapter 6 examines the evolving inspection framework and the ways in which institutions, agencies and organizations such as awarding bodies have been responsible for monitoring the assurance and enhancement of quality in FE.

Hodgson and Spours (1997) argue that all these policies are set within what they term a 'weak framework approach', because much of the emphasis is placed on individuals rather than examining systemic barriers that prevent people engaging with learning opportunities, or weak systems, which do not fully attempt to draw together the range of agencies, such as employment, social welfare and education, responsible for adults. Some of the policy strands outlined above have been the subject of more 'joined-up thinking' than others. The social exclusion strand appears to employ a more targeted approach than, for example, the quality approach. Continuing tension exists around the qualifications framework and the funding of learning, which relies on employer involvement, particularly for higher-level qualifications.

As noted in Chapter 1, a deliberative policy analysis would expect tensions to exist and would predict that people will define the issues differently, therefore arguing over the best way forward. The following chapters will examine these tensions, which all stem from the overarching question, 'how do we ensure that people today are knowledgeable, skilled and socially included in ways that will not damage other people or our environment, in a society that has to compete globally?'

3 Success for All

'Education is the best economic policy we have.'
(Tony Blair, *The Learning Age*)

To create an infrastructure that would implement the vision of *The Learning Age*, in 1999 the government produced a White Paper, *Learning to Succeed*. This outlined proposals for the education and training of both young people and adults. The White Paper began the strategy for rationalizing post-16 education and training through the creation of one national and numerous regional Skills Councils. The core of the framework was to build a 'new culture of learning and aspiration which will underpin national competitiveness and personal prosperity, encourage creativity and innovation and help build a more cohesive society' (DfEE 1999: 13).

Why was this White Paper written? By the end of the last century, the UK was lagging behind most of the other major economies in productivity, and despite good performance by highly qualified people, it lagged behind its competitors at intermediate and technical levels (below level 4 in the national qualifications framework). The challenge was to increase skills levels to match those of the country's competitors, and to do this by achieving a 'step change' in the aspirations of individuals, tackling social exclusion in the education system, and focusing on employability, rather than employment in the labour force (DfEE 1999: 12). The White Paper argued that the government could realize its vision through a new partnership which would drive up standards and performance by removing structural barriers within the system. Standing still was 'not an option' (DfEE 1999: 15).

Structural change was necessary, because there was too much

duplication, confusion and bureaucracy in the system, an absence of effective coordination and strategic planning, and insufficient focus on skill and employer needs nationally, regionally and locally. The system at the time fell far short of the principles set out in *The Learning Age* (DfEE 1998).

The decision, then, was to create a different structure of provision through the creation of a national quango, the Learning and Skills Council (LSC). The government used legislation to achieve such far-reaching change in the Learning and Skills Act, which received royal assent in 2000. Nearly every aspect of policy addressing the work of FE has stemmed from the principles outlined in *The Learning Age* (1998), taken forward in *Learning to Succeed* (1999), and subsequently operationalized through the *Success for All* strategy (2002). This chapter starts by examining these overarching policies. The themes arising from the aims of these strategies, such as widening participation, improving quality, fostering a culture of lifelong learning, as well as implementing structural changes in provision, notably creating a system which addressed the learning needs of 14–19-year-olds, are discussed in the following chapters.

The Learning and Skills Act

The Learning and Skills Act came into force in April 2001 and as a result the national Learning and Skills Council (LSC), the biggest quango in the country, was created. The LSC is a non-departmental public body, with responsibility for the planning and allocation of nearly £9 billion of public money for over 7 million learners. It is responsible for the funding, planning and quality assurance of further education colleges, school sixth forms, work-based training for young people, workforce development, adult and community learning, information, advice and guidance for adults and education business links. The national council originally operated through 47 local 'arms' with responsibility for coordinating local plans, building on the previous government initiative, Learning Partnerships. These 47 local councils have recently become more regionalized to reflect the nature of other regional activities. Connexions was created in 2001 to provide an integrated youth support service. The responsibility for work-based learning for adults was transferred to the Employment Service in 2001 in order to provide a more integrated service of support for unemployed adults. The setting up of the national LSC and its 47 regional counterparts was a bold development in the government's strategy to ensure that all those over the age of compulsory schooling could have access to, and benefit from, education and training opportunities.

The council had a number of key priorities, including:

- Delivering the vision of *The Learning Age* by fostering a culture and commitment to learning through partnership working, and to fulfil the duty to encourage participation in learning.
- Making a contribution to the economy in terms of productivity and competitiveness by updating skills.
- Improving the basic skills of adults and young people.
- Raising standards in post-16 learning and ensuring excellence in teaching and training.
- Drawing up an equal opportunities strategy and action plan with targets and performance indicators to tackle under-representation and under-achievement.
- Building a single organization with a cohesive structure, common culture and common goals and objectives.

These priorities are likely to have changed by the time you read this chapter. For more information, you may wish to consult the DfES website, www.dfes.gov.uk/post16 or the LSC website, www.lsc.gov.uk.

FE and Centres of Vocational Excellence

One of the priorities that government identified for the learning and skills sector was to raise standards, a 'mantra' in public sector policymaking at the time. In 2000, David Blunkett, as Secretary of State for Education, defined a new vision for FE in his announcement that there would be funding to establish Centres of Vocational Excellence (COVEs). The key policy document *Colleges for Excellence and Innovation* outlined four objectives.

- To provide high and improving standards of education for 16–19-year-olds, ensuring increased participation and achievement on broad and balanced programmes of study.
- To play the leading role in providing the skills the economy needs at craft, technician and equivalent levels through initial technical and vocational education for young people and skills upgrading or re-training for adults.
- To widen participation in learning, enabling adults to acquire the basic skills they need for employability, effective citizenship and enjoyment of learning.
- To provide a ladder of opportunity to higher education with a key focus on foundation degrees, built on partnerships and networks with higher education institutions and with learndirect to share and make widely available learning resources (DfEE 2000: 4–5).

FE, then, took centre stage in the government's twin aims of economic success and social inclusion.

Success for All

The implementation of the aims of the government's Learning and Skills Act, itself a response to the White Paper *Learning to Succeed* (1999), was set up through a change programme called *Success for All*, designed to 'transform quality and responsiveness across the learning and skills sector' (Success for All website, November 2003). The programme was launched in November 2002 by the then newly appointed Education Secretary, Charles Clarke. At the time, FE was facing what Besley describes as one of its 'regular funding crises' (Besley 2003: 3) and the announcement that an extra £1.5 billion over three years was being made available caught the attention of media and FE staff alike. Besley has argued that this strategy was a genuine attempt to help reinvent FE, which always had a perception problem:

'Under funded, under valued, unloved and still stuck with the Cinderella tag, what was needed was a new gleaming, demand led, technology infused and community driven sector.' (Besley 2003: 3)

There are four key themes in *Success for All*:

- meeting needs and improving choice
- putting teaching, training and learning at the heart of what we do
- developing the leaders, teachers, lecturers, trainers and support staff of the future
- developing a framework for quality and success.

Strategic Area Reviews (StARs) were set up in 2003 to help address theme one, 'meeting needs and improving choice'. Each local LSC was asked to carry out a review of its provision by the then minister responsible for FE, Alan Johnson, and to 'think as innovatively as possible during the mission review'. The reviews had to undertake complex analyses of regional skills, budgets and planning models, all having to fit into an ever-changing policy framework, as government continued to produce more reports, White Papers and legislation. A particular policy steer has been from the publication in 2003 of the government's skills strategy White Paper, *Realising Our Potential: Individuals, Employers, Nation* (DfES 2003), published by the DfES, Department of Trade and Industry (DTI), Department for Work and Pensions (DWP) and the Treasury.

Theme two, 'putting teaching, training and learning at the heart of what we do', began to take shape through the establishment of the Standards Unit. Created in 2002, it was set up to help foster good practice in pedagogy. Pilots were set up to develop teaching and learning materials, which have, at the time of writing in 2005, already been 'rolled out' in four areas: business studies, construction, entry to employment and science. In 2004, four more areas (land-based studies, health and social care, mathematics and ICT) began to be the focus of the 'standards treatment'.

This work has been particularly influenced by a damning report by Ofsted on initial teacher training in FE, particularly in relation to the lack of subject-specialist training, and poor basic skills among nearly a third of tutors across the institutions inspected in 2003. At the same time, another government initiative, the creation of Sector Skills Councils, is now beginning to impact on the FE sector, after the Lifelong Learning Sector Skills Council (LLUK) was established in 2004. Previous attempts to address the quality of teaching and learning in FE through the creation of the Further Education National Training Organization (FENTO) have been further developed, but are, again, subject to the government review of initial teacher training, and a different strategy to ensure quality staff has been proposed, with the creation of a licence to practice, not dissimilar to qualified teacher status (QTS) in schools.

This aspect of the Success for All strategy is very much linked to issues of quality (covered in Chapter 6), but readers will be familiar by now with the way in which one strategy is affected by another, and how the pace of change means that it is sometimes difficult to remember which policy any new initiative stems from!

The third strand of *Success for All* is 'developing the leaders, teachers, lecturers, trainers and support staff of the future'. Workforce development strategy is primarily the focus of work by the Standards Unit. Following the DfES consultation on FE initial teacher training in November 2003, recommendations were made to create a different qualification structure, with a passport to teach arising from an introductory programme (not dissimilar to the original Stage One of a City and Guilds quali-fication), and a second tier of training which could be taken over five years, leading to a licence to practice. There is an interim target that 90 per cent of full-time and 60 per cent of part-time teachers should be qualified to teach in FE by 2006.

Alongside the development of teaching and learning, there is a focus on the managers and leaders and how they, too, need support to function effectively and contribute to the goals of Success for All. A Centre for Excellence in Leadership (CEL) was created in October 2003. Modelled along the lines of the successful Leadership Development Framework and National Professional Qualification for Headship (NPQH), initiatives of the National College for School Leadership to professionally develop head teachers in schools, CEL has a remit to offer support for principals, deputy principals and aspiring principals.

The fourth strand, 'developing a framework for quality and success', has been the subject of LSC circulars outlining a change to FE funding, introducing block funding rather than the bureaucratic annual funding mechanism that had been inherited from the FEFC. Indeed, this strand is linked to a different government initiative, the Bureaucracy Task Force (BTF), which was set up to reduce the enormous bureaucracy in the learning and skills sector, something the Foster Review in 2005 also addressed. The development of longer-term planning and analysis of local learning and business needs does not escape the mainstay of government monitoring systems – targets. However, on a positive note, by 2003, success rates for all qualifications in colleges rose from 59 per cent in 2001 to 65 per cent in 2003. There was a fall in colleges inspected as 'inadequate' from 14 per cent to 10 per cent between 2001 and 2003. Twenty-five providers had been awarded Learning and Skills Beacon status. Success for All, then, even after its first full year of operation, was delivering on some of the targets outlined in the strategy.

Realising our Potential

The Skills Strategy White Paper, *Realising our Potential*, 2003, was a major piece of government policymaking which drew together four government departments. It did not aim to introduce new initiatives, but attempted to integrate what already existed and to create a stronger focus. The paper identified five key areas for action:

- employers' needs to become centre stage
- help employers use skills to achieve more ambitious longer-term business success
- motivate and support more learners to re-engage in learning
- make colleges and training providers more responsive to employers' and learners' needs
- better joint working across government and the public services in a new Skills Alliance.

By now, the context within which this White Paper was drawn up comprised not only the historic weaknesses in productivity and a skills gap, but also the European context of needing to meet the five economic tests for UK membership of the single currency. This required the contribution of lifelong learning, which in turn required input from FE. The challenge set out by the White Paper was to create a coherent policy framework that supported frontline delivery and developed an education and training system focused on the needs of employers and learners: in other words, one that was demand-led rather than provider-led.

To achieve this, the training market was opened up to include private, voluntary and community providers in the funding mechanism in ways in which they were able to attract 'hard-to-reach' learners. Partnerships mechanisms were emphasized, for example the Skills Alliance between government (notably the DfES and the DTI), the Confederation of British Industry (CBI), the Trades Union Congress (TUC) and the Small Business Council.

The agenda was redistributive, so that priority was given to adults without a full level 2 qualification, and funding would be provided to enable this group to participate in learning opportunities for no fee. Adults could qualify for a learning grant, modelled on an Education Maintenance Allowance (EMA), which had been introduced for young people in 1999 as a pilot. EMAs were introduced for adults in 2004. Interestingly, there was a commitment to safeguard wider learning opportunities for culture, leisure, community and personal fulfilment. This commitment was something the policy eventually compromised through funding decisions made in 2005 when there was not enough funding to cover the level 2 entitlement, and all other provision was consequently expected to recoup income from increased fees. By July 2005, colleges were being forced to pulp their adult learning prospectuses as they could no longer sustain provision, given the massive decrease in funding for this area of their work.

The government continued its commitment to Modern Apprenticeships (MAs), to developing a credit framework for adults, and it identified ICT as a third basic skill and hence part of the priority for funded learning opportunities.

The White Paper caused a frenzy of response, particularly from the post-compulsory education and training sector, which was at the forefront of ensuring that the aims could be achieved. The July edition of *Adults Learning* drew together a range of responses including comments categorizing the paper as 'mould breaking', 'joined-up thinking', a 'merry-go-round' and even a 'missed opportunity'. One commentator argued that there was too much in the strategy, and that the government should 'prioritize no more than three objectives and drive them home' (Sherlock 2003: 9). There was general agreement, however, that there did not seem to be a mechanism for turning strategy into action. This was particularly evident regarding the role of employers, which, despite being outlined in a section on their responsibilities, was still conceptualized on the basis of 'voluntarism rules OK' (Rainbird 2003: 12).

However, the decision to publish the paper on behalf of four government departments demonstrated a genuine attempt to create a coherent strategy that would be understood and 'owned' by those who held the purse strings and the power. If we examine the way in which education has been labelled by government, we can see that it has moved from the Department of Education and Science (DES) to the Department for Education and Employment (DfEE) and now the Department for Education and Skills (DfES). The link with the Department of Trade and Industry (DTI) and the Department for Work and Pensions (DWP) demonstrates how the world of work and that of unemployment needs to be considered when developing strategies for workforce development, ostensibly under the aegis of a department responsible for education.

A number of initiatives have emerged from this White Paper. The establishment of Frameworks for Regional Employment and Skills Action (FRESAs) was intended to help guide the allocation of funds by local LSCs to employers, and in particular to help support the delivery of an increase in level 3 qualifications. Non-award-bearing programmes of learning were to be funded by agreement with government and the LSC, based on expenditure at the time, but with an agreed minimum figure.

The White Paper took account of additional reviews commissioned by government, including the review of qualifications through the establishment of the Tomlinson Review of 14–19 qualifications, a review of science, engineering, mathematics and technology initiatives, the Smith review of post-14 mathematics, and a review of generic employability skills and how these can be developed in 14–19-year-olds. The government had just created a new higher education qualification, the foundation degree, which aimed to address skills shortages at higher levels.

One of the interesting components of *Realising our Potential* is the emphasis on entitlement. As anyone not qualified to level 2 (the equivalent of five GCSEs at grades A–C) is guaranteed free learning, with an adult learning grant of up to £30 per week, the government set in train a policy that has required a number of activities to ensure that it can be successful, for example the need to create a unique learner number, so that people can be tracked through the system. As noted above, the consequences of the policy of entitlement, ironically, is that other groups of people become disenfranchized, because the funding is not there to support their learning. At the time, then, that employers were being asked to participate in the strategy to help develop the workforce, if their employees needed education and training at higher levels, they were given less financial encouragement. As the Learning and Skills Development Agency (LSDA) noted, the White Paper did not flinch from the consequences: if total funds are limited, some learners would get more support, others would get less. To pay for the higher-level qualifications, fee income from employers and from those learners not in priority groups needed to increase (Fletcher 2003: 1).

The strategy outlined in *Realising our Potential* was updated in 2005 by the publication of the Skills White Paper, *Skills: Getting on in Business, Getting on at Work*. The paper builds on the original national strategy of *Realising our Potential*, but there is now greater emphasis on level 3 qualifications with a 'clear ladder of progression', and the idea that there needs to be a broker who can negotiate training and business support for employers.

There are four key aspects. First, National Employer Training Programmes (NETPs), which will offer free training at basic skills, level 2 and access to learning levels, are set to begin in

2006/7 with a total of £355m of Treasury funding, the Treasury being the government department that is particularly interested in this initiative. NETPs follow Employer Training Pilots, another Treasury initiative, launched in 2002 and administered through local LSCs. On evaluating these pilots it became apparent that brokers played a key role in 'taking the offer to employers and animating demand'. Thus, in the 2005 White Paper, brokers will play an important role. Brokers are able to choose which provider should deliver the training, forcing FE and training providers back into the competitive arena from which they have only just begun to emerge.

The second key aspect is the realization that skills need to be raised to level 3, even though the current funding mechanism is still one of entitlement for level 2, thus squeezing provision at level 3, as employers and individuals continue to be reluctant to pay the extra fees required. Although by autumn 2004, 50.8 per cent of adults were qualified to level 3 or above, a rise of 7.75 per cent over the past ten years, the most significant skills gaps exist at this level. The White Paper, though, only provides funding with the expectation that employers (who of course will benefit from the additional skills their employees gain) should pay for the training, but helped by the NETP scheme.

The third aspect is the proposal to set up a network of Skills Academies, 'one for each major sector of the economy established in partnerships with employers in the sector'. It is expected that there will be twelve Skills Academies providing training for 16–19-year-olds during the next three years. These Academies will be co-sponsored and co-funded by employers.

Finally, the Skills White Paper wants employers to be involved in Sector Skills Agreements, which aim to bring employers together voluntarily so that they can tackle the skills needs of their sector.

Perhaps a cynical view, expressed by Besley, is worth repeating here.

'Brokers will no doubt prove very useful but it still seems a bit perverse to have created such a complicated system that results in users needing to "hire" someone to guide them through it.' (Besley 2005a: 2)

However, there is a clear intent by government to improve workforce skills and, increasingly, an acknowledgement that this can't happen without motivating staff, through incentives that also involve employers, and ultimately by ensuring that vocational and educational systems can help provide the 'right skills' quickly enough. The idea that social inclusion can be aided through progress in the labour market is now acknowledged as being dependent not just on individuals, but also on other stakeholders, particularly employers, who need to invest in training, alongside the government, through the vast learning and skills sector.

At the time of writing, the latest Skills White Paper is out for consultation. However, the learning and skills sector has a set of strategies directed at creating a culture of lifelong learning across school, college, university and the workplace. There is an agenda to drive up standards, to introduce opportunities for learning through technology, to develop the workforce, and to ensure that the system is responsive on a demand-led rather than provider-led basis. Specific areas of activity, such as those concentrating on the basic skills of literacy, language, numeracy and technology, are dealt with in a separate strategy, the Skills for Life Strategy, outlined in the following chapter. The Treasury and Cabinet Office are prime sources of agenda setting and, through the increasing use of technology, consultations with stakeholders are conducted on almost every initiative that is launched.

Having identified very briefly some of the main policy moments in the past five years, it is important to return to the policy analysis menu and begin to examine the consequences of these initiatives and, in particular, the role of FE managers in their implementation.

Targets, targets, targets

How does the Success for All strategy and its linked initiatives measure up? The government approach to monitoring is through the establishment of targets, which are then analysed and usually revised. Criticisms of this target-driven culture abound (Skidmore 2003; Goldstein 2006). Handy describes the

'Macnamara Fallacy', whereby measuring what can be measured is acceptable, but ignoring what can't be measured is not only 'blindness' but can lead to a situation where what can't be measured is deemed unimportant, which is 'suicide' (Handy 1994: 219). Thus, in the FE sector, it has become relatively easy to create targets that measure numbers of learners, numbers of those who achieve qualifications, those who stay on a programme, and the distance they have travelled from starting a programme with existing qualifications to where they complete the programme. What is much harder to measure is how much confidence has been gained, how much more socially aware and active people have become, how much healthier, mentally and physically, they have become and also to what long-term effects their learning has contributed. Despite evidence from research on the wider benefits of learning (Schuller et al. 2004), the sector continues to be asked to return information, and to meet targets, which are 'proxy' measures of learning. Skills for Life, in particular, has targets that are hotly contested by practitioners, and the performance indicator, the achievement of a basic skills qualification, is not necessarily an indication that a person's basic skill has improved (of which more in Chapter 4):

> 'What is purchased is never learning itself, but some proxy for it. The "proxies" that are used to trigger the funding provided by funding councils may not be the same as those which an individual would wish to "contract" to purchase from a provider. Whichever proxies are used, they will tend to emphasise only one aspect of what goes to make up effective learning. Other aspects may need to be protected via the work of inspectorates and regulatory bodies.' (Stanton 2000: 10)

Goldstein identifies the dangers of 'high stakes' target setting, in which individuals adapt their behaviour to maximize perceived rewards. This is a rational response to external pressures, but it leads to highly dysfunctional consequences (Goldstein 2006). The testing of children in England can lead to demotivation and anxiety amongst pupils, particularly those who are low achievers, to setting targets that are difficult to attain, and potentially to resignations of ministers responsible for setting them. Luckily, ministers responsible for lifelong learning have a particularly short shelf life, and most have moved on before their lack of achievement on targets catches up with them!

Policy analysis of Success for All

The pillars of lifelong learning, economic competitiveness and social inclusion have been fairly unequally distributed in government policy subsequently. As Hyland and Merrill argue, although the FE sector can be said to represent the 'heart and soul of New Labour's general lifelong learning policy for the PCET sector' (Hyland and Merrill 2003: 20), the terrain is deeply contested, and the increasing focus on economic competitiveness is to be achieved through the 'soft objective' (Field 2000) of placing responsibility on individuals, communities and various stakeholders.

If we return to the ways in which policy can be analysed, simply in terms of policy stages, we can see that the frenetic activity of policy, strategy and resulting initiatives to address 'problems' in education and training is actually linked to an overall project of ensuring economic competitiveness, with a slightly less clear aim to increase social inclusion. We can see that policies are building on each other, and that there have also been attempts to monitor and evaluate the implementation of policy ideas through the use of pilots. There is consultation and debate resulting from White Papers and legislation. Interestingly, much policy that emanates from government is achieved through department dictat using White Papers, not through legislation. Funding is a key policy lever for affecting change.

A stagist policy analysis belies the tensions and disputes that the sector has to manage. If we take a critical discourse approach of deliberative policy analysis (DPA), we can begin to see that government is adopting a 'charm offensive' on the one hand, but is very quick to scold on the other. The wording in recent White Papers is one of exhortation, and the quangos and agencies that have been created to implement strategy are subject to strict control by spin doctors. Information dissemination is carefully controlled. For example, the latest

Standards Unit Newsletter discusses the White Paper in terms of a benign government wanting to help:

'The Government is clear about the need for change and the priorities, but it does not want to overburden the system with change. The aim is to fashion the system around the needs of learners and employers, but the Government doesn't want to prescribe every step. Given variety in local circumstances, the changing nature of society and the economy, and the ongoing development of learning technologies, to do so would be foolish.' (DfES 2005a: 3)

So what does this mean for a college manager?

If we take the deliberative policy analysis (DPA) approach, we would expect to find tensions and dispute, and these are indeed central to understanding how the sector operates. It is this approach that will become most apparent in the ensuing chapters. But what does this mean for the 'people on the ground', the managers in a local FE college who are faced with implementing the Success for All strategy? They have to ensure that their staff are fully trained, that they meet targets in recruitment, retention and achievement, that they work with employers, and that all programmes are of good quality, with evidence to demonstrate this.

Perhaps the most obvious implication of the policies outlined above is that managers do need to keep up to date with the latest government policymaking. This can be done by reading the educational press, particularly the *Guardian* on Tuesdays, and *The Times Education Supplement* with its *FE Focus*. There are websites for information about various strands of the Success for All strategy, listed in Useful Websites (p. 115). There are email groups that circulate news, such as the Skills and Education Network Newsletter (SENET), and this provides links to government information and websites, summarizes the latest facts and figures and policy reviews and provides information about forthcoming events.

The second thing for college managers to do is to engage critically with any particular policy that will affect them, identifying the effects it will have on their staff, learners and institution. This does not mean that managers simply have to implement a new initiative unquestioningly. As noted in Chapter 1, critical reflection on what the policy appears to address, what its unintended consequences are likely to be, and what likelihood there is of achieving the aims, provides a more proactive approach to policy enaction.

4 Skills for Life

'Literacy and economic "enlightenment" seem cast in a symbiotic relationship, a straightforward logic within which one's skills portfolio – of which literacy skills are an important aspect – is directly and unproblematically linked to earning capacity. The comprehensiveness of the current Skills for Life initiative can be seen as a managerialist response to this.' (Herrington and Kendall 2005: xiv)

A major focus of the government's agenda to be economically competitive, and for social inclusion, is to ensure that adults in the UK have a basic level of literacy, numeracy and language skills which will equip them to participate in work and the community and to function effectively in social life. Why is this necessary? To answer this question, we need to look back over the past three decades to a time when it was assumed that most people could read, write and use mathematics, could speak English fluently, and had learnt to do all of these at school. As adults, they might be a bit rusty on some aspects of writing or of mathematics, but they could not possibly have trouble reading or speaking English, unless they had learning difficulties. It was quite a shock, then, in 1975 when the BBC programme *On the Move*, which was broadcast on Sunday evenings, showed a lorry driver learning to read and write, and which then gave a phone number for people to call if they, too, had problems with their reading and writing. There was also a call for people to volunteer to help other adults improve their literacy. At the time, it was estimated that two million people had difficulties with literacy.

Today, the estimate is that five million adults have trouble with literacy, and nine million with numeracy. Of course, these estimates do not demonstrate a decline since the 1970s, but rather that there is a greater awareness of basic skills, as adult literacy, language and numeracy (ALLN) are now called. The increased estimates also demonstrate that there are national and international comparisons of basic skills for young people and adults, and that the government has increasingly focused attention on this area in the past ten years.

A history of basic skills had been examined by Hamilton (1996) and more recently updated by Hamilton and Hillier (2006). This chapter develops the 'story' from 2000 onwards, focusing on policy development. To do this, it is necessary to examine one major policy moment, in 1999, when a report by Sir Claus Moser was published. His report, *A Fresh Start: Improving Literacy and Numeracy*, brought into the public eye the 'shocking' state of affairs that an estimated seven million people could not operate at the level of an eleven-year-old, as far as reading was concerned. The report makes sobering reading. Research (for example Bynner and Parsons 1997) has indicated that at least 20 per cent of adults in the country have low levels of basic skills to the extent that they cannot read simple instructions or calculate a simple arithmetic sum. This low level of basic skills is linked to many indices of poverty, including poor housing, poor health and unemployment. That is not to say that all people who have difficulty with literacy are poor, or that all poor people must have low literacy and numeracy levels. However, there is evidence that low levels of basic skills prevents people from being economically successful and can lead to social exclusion, thus creating a downward spiral which is hard to stop. Moser's report argued that to achieve an inclusive and economically successful society it is important that people should have a level of basic skills that enables them to be employed.

The figures for this report were informed by two main sources: a British longitudinal study and an international survey. The longitudinal study, the National Child Development Survey (NCDS), has tracked the lives of all children born in one week in March 1958. As so much is known about this cohort, it is possible to identify trends, including the fact that those with poor literacy and numeracy skills tend to have poorer health, tend to be less likely to be fully employed, and are also more likely to have families with similar problems (Bynner and Parsons 1997).

To understand why Moser was asked to lead an inquiry into adult basic skills, we have to look to the European Union. Any European Union paper on adult vocational education and training, or lifelong learning, has included addressing basic skills as a priority since the mid-1990s. The European Union *Memorandum on Lifelong Learning* (2000), for example, makes a clear correlation between poor basic skills, lack of economic competitiveness and social exclusion. An International Adult Literacy Survey (IALS) showed that Britain was by no means in the lead in terms of its placement in an international rank order of literacy skills (OECD 1997, 2000). Nine countries (France, Germany, Ireland, the Netherlands, Sweden, Canada, Poland, Switzerland and the US) participated in IALS, although France withdrew from the reporting stage. The aim of the survey was to provide comparison levels of 'prose', 'document' and 'quantitative' literacy by using the same measuring instrument. Three thousand people in each country were tested in their homes (Goldstein 2006). Governments included in the survey began to identify strategies to address the levels of basic skills in their countries. The UK, like many of its counterparts, created a particular policy focus on ALLN. Westernized countries are also the subject of ongoing research by the Organization for Economic Cooperation and Development (OECD) on comparisons between countries and on indices of social inclusion and economic success. The results continue to influence national policymaking.

The results of IALS, and the way the survey was conducted, were criticized by Goldstein (2006) because they did not necessarily represent what people can actually do in terms of literacy and numeracy. However, the survey provided a huge impetus to government activity in the UK. The four countries of the UK responded differently to the same issue, but this chapter will focus on England, the policy decisions that have been taken as a result of IALS, and the Moser Report.

As with the other reports, Moser identified that action was needed, both in terms of creating learning opportunities for people, which would be more accessible than previous attempts to resource learning opportunities, and ensuring that those who create, deliver and manage learning programmes are qualified and supported to do so. In schools there is a national agenda to raise levels of literacy and numeracy, through a literacy and numeracy strategy that includes a 'literacy hour' in all primary schools. This idea was translated into the national curriculum for learners so that all adults, regardless of where they learn, should be following a curriculum that is consistent and coherent across the country.

The main recommendations of Moser were to:

- develop a national target for increasing participation in basic skills programmes for adults
- increase levels of basic skills by raising functional literacy in England from 80 per cent to 90 per cent and functional numeracy from 60 per cent to 70 per cent
- increase numbers of professionally qualified teachers of adult literacy, numeracy and ESOL.

Moser identified that, despite the motivation of tutors and committed partners in addressing adult basic skills, there was no national coordination of provision, no national standards or agreed pedagogy, and that there were poorly trained teachers, with ineffective management, poor inspection grades, employers who were not engaged and learners who were reluctant. Needless to say, such conclusions drew heavy criticism from the field, particularly as a range of qualifications for basic skills tutors had been in place since 1990, including the widely used City and Guilds 9281 series for people just entering teaching on a one-to-one basis, along with the generic teaching qualification, the City and Guilds 730 series. However, the report provided huge impetus in securing funding for a strategy that would address the issues raised by Moser.

As a result of the Moser Report, the government created its new strategy, Skills for Life (Sk4L), in 2001. The focus of the strategy was to improve the basic skills of adults by:

- increasing demand
- raising capacity

- improving quality
- increasing learner achievement.

The key priorities were to engage learners, raise standards and coordinate planning and delivery.

Engaging learners would be achieved by:

- giving all adults an entitlement to free literacy, numeracy and language training that reflected their needs and was available when and where they needed it
- establishing a clear route to qualifications that help learners and teachers understand what is needed to progress
- launching and sustaining a promotional strategy targeted at those who could improve their skills and those who could support them.

Raising standards would be achieved by:

- establishing national standards, screening and diagnostic assessment, a national core curriculum and new national tests, and commissioning new learning materials to support them
- enhancing the status of teachers by introducing professional qualifications for all literacy and numeracy teachers from September 2001
- improving inspection arrangements to provide a rigorous and robust quality framework.

Coordinating planning and delivery would be achieved by:

- setting targets and increasing funding so that all providers receive funds for learners following a literacy or numeracy course
- targeting key priority groups and making sure all parts of government are focused on common goals
- establishing regional pathfinder areas to test how best to increase retention and achievement rates. A centre of research will commission more analysis including a baseline survey of need.

A significant amount of funding was found for the initiative. In 2000, £241 million was spent on literacy and numeracy by the

DfEE. This funding increased to £403 million in 2003, a real terms increase of over 55 per cent over the three-year period. The National Audit Office estimated that by 2006 £3.7 billion would have been spent on implementing the Sk4L Strategy (NAO 2004: 1).

The DfES created the Adult Basic Skills and Strategy Unit (ABSSU, now known as the Skills for Life Strategy Unit) to oversee the implementation of its recommendations. Skills for Life is being acted upon through a variety of provision including the learndirect initiative, family learning projects, union-funded programmes, quality standards in basic skills provision, accreditation and training for basic skills teachers and organizers and in qualifications in basic skills for learners. There is hardly any form of education and training for adults that does not address the need to develop the basic skills of their participants somewhere in its activities.

The national curriculum identified a series of levels that would fit within the national framework of qualifications. Thus, there were the two main levels, one and two, that were equivalent to GCSEs and vocational qualifications. However, given that basic skills had to be offered at levels below level one, there were three 'entry levels'. Entry level one is the lowest level, and is the equivalent of a national curriculum level for 5- to 7-year-old children, entry level two is equivalent to national curriculum level 2 for 7- to 9-year-old children, and entry level three is equivalent to national curriculum level three for 9- to 11-year-olds. Someone with entry level one should be able to write a short message or choose the correct coins for a public telephone, whereas someone with entry level three could use a touch-screen information point or pay a household bill.

The Sk4L Strategy was a pragmatic attempt to find a 'solution' to the basic skills 'problem'. There was recognition that learners may have had poor learning experiences in the past, and that it was important to find ways to motivate them to learn again. There needed to be quality provision and there needed to be impact as a result of learning. How would this be measured? The method favoured by the current government is to set targets. Thus, if there has to be an increase in the number of people improving their basic skills, there needs to be a target of how many people should do so by a set date. This begs the question of what an indicator of 'improving basic skills' is. The decision to create a national curriculum meant that it would be possible to test how well people performed against that curriculum, and hence led to the idea that testing would provide the information required to monitor how well people were improving their basic skills. It was a short step towards deciding that the true measure of achieving a target to improve people's basic skills was to create a national testing framework.

National tests were introduced with Certificates in Adult Literacy and Numeracy at levels 1 and 2. The tests have been heavily critiqued (Lavender *et al.* 2004), particularly because the literacy tests originally included no writing at all (Mace 2002). Funding is linked to achievement of the national qualifications, and hence there are strong incentives for providers to ensure that learners engage with qualifications, and therefore participate in a heavy testing framework.

The government targets for adults to gain basic skills qualifications were: by 2004, 750,000 adults should have gained an equivalent level 2 qualification in basic skills; and by 2007 this number should have reached 1.5 million. A further target has been set for 2.25 million adults by 2010. The 2004 target has been reached, but this includes learners who were already in the system. The 'hard-to-reach' learners will be much more difficult to engage. In 2004, the National Audit Office (NAO) estimated that up to 55 per cent of 16–19-year-olds had literacy skills below level 2, and 78 per cent had numeracy skills below level 2 (equivalent to a pass at GCSE at grades A* to C). The figure was very similar for adults aged 20–65.

How to create demand? The newly created ABSSU launched a media campaign, *Get On*, which featured gremlins to help people recognize the ways they avoid showing their lack of basic skills, and to encourage them to do something about their continual fear of being found out. A series of short television advertisements appeared on ITV, along with posters and printed material. The campaigns were reinforced at local level by local Learning and Skills Councils and by learndirect. The gremlin characters were successful in that they had a high rate of public recognition and almost 300,000 people contacted the learndirect national advice line following the first campaign (NAO 2004: 39). Approximately 26 per cent of those who contacted the advice line went on to take up learning opportunities. A second campaign started in 2004, and further media exposure is planned.

Skills for Life is not only directed at learners. In addition to the national curriculum for learners, there is a set of standards for practitioners, underpinning qualifications at levels 3 and 4. These standards for literacy, numeracy and ESOL include subject-specific knowledge in addition to the more generic issues of teaching and learning, as outlined by the FENTO standards. It was recognized that adult literacy and numeracy work had low status, and that teachers were not always fully supported in their professional development.

By now, the FENTO standards had been created to help direct the professional development of teaching staff in FE. A further set of standards was created which specifically addressed what literacy, numeracy or ESOL specialists should know in order to teach basic skills. Chapter 6 discusses the generic issues around teacher training, but the creation of standards for basic skills is particularly interesting, given that there had been a general disquiet expressed by Ofsted about the lack of specialist development for FE teachers in 2003 (Ofsted 2003b). The new qualifications were set at level 4 in the qualification framework, approximately equivalent to a first-year undergraduate programme, and were available from September 2002.

The incentive to help providers enable their staff to gain qualifications was undertaken through the Learning and Skills Quality Initiative in 2003, in which a modular professional development programme was introduced, so that both new and experienced teachers could update their knowledge. A further set of qualifications was introduced at level 3 for people who support literacy and numeracy learners, as well as at level two for people who undertake assessment of learning needs and give guidance.

One outcome of the professional development aspect of Skills for Life has been the creation of professional development centres. In London, for example, South Bank University houses a centre for supporting numeracy, which is run by the Literacy and Language Unit (LLU). The DfES supported training for vocational tutors and has commissioned an embedded materials project, which released its first set of materials in 2004.

The DfES funded a national research and development centre (NRDC) in spring 2002 to help underpin knowledge about how best to help adults acquire basic skills. The centre works with practitioners as researchers, as well as undertaking its own research. It has been particularly active in supporting practitioners, and has reported on a number of research projects that have tested new ideas and approaches to learning, has identified international best practice and has supported practitioner research projects that help bring the notion of critical inquiry to people who teach basic skills (see www.nrdc.org.uk).

Policy analysis of Skills for Life

Why was Sk4L so successful in winning government interest? The introduction to the strategy by the then Minister of State for Education, David Blunkett, gives an indication:

> 'A shocking 7 million adults in England cannot read and write at the level we would expect of an 11-year-old. Even more have problems with numbers. The cost to the country as a whole could be as high as £10 billion a year. The cost to people's personal lives is incalculable. People with low basic skills earn an average £50,000 less over their working lives, are more likely to have health problems or to turn to crime. These people, and their children, risk being cut off from the advantages of a world increasingly linked through information and technology. A fair and prosperous society cannot be built on such insecure foundations.' (Blunkett in DfES 2001)

Within this paragraph, we can see that a financial cost is calculated, to the country as a whole, as well as to individuals. The link to poverty and crime is made, and the notion that fairness and prosperity are unlikely to be achieved because of a link with low basic skills is claimed. No government would risk doing nothing if social disorder (crime) and economic decline (cost to the country) were to result.

Further analysis of the discourse of the Skills for Life strategy shows that strong, threatening language is used. There are 'disastrous' consequences for the country with a 'huge burden' on society (p. 6). People with low basic skills suffer from 'inertia and fatalism' which are the 'chief enemies' of the government (p. 7). People with low basic skills 'suffer' (p. 8). The government response is to create 'bold and imaginative' policies.

The impact of Skills for Life

Given the level of funding, and the profile of government attention to adult basic skills, it is not surprising that there has been strong monitoring of progress.

An inspection of basic skills by Ofsted (2003c) identified a lack of progress amongst learners, with high drop-out rates, poor quality of assessment of learners' progress and achievement, and poor setting of targets by managers. Ofsted also identified that there is good practice in particular areas, but that, in some circumstances, people who are able to motivate young learners, for example through Job Centre Plus and other agencies outwith the education institutions, are not necessarily able to teach basic skills themselves.

The National Audit Office report a year later found little evidence of the impact of progress on the quality of learning, and identified that there is a widespread shortage of qualified teaching staff (NAO 2004: 49). One area in which this is proving to be particularly contentious is in numeracy. In the past, many numeracy tutors have been recruited from literacy teaching. Learners who are grappling with form filling, for example, or timetables, are using numeracy as well as literacy, and it is sometimes quite difficult to artificially divide a learning session into literacy or numeracy. However, because tutors are teaching numeracy, this does not mean that they have a high level of mathematics knowledge, nor that they are qualified to teach mathematics. Being asked to meet the level four qualification in the FENTO standards is threatening to such tutors, and there is a danger that many will simply withdraw from teaching, rather than undertake the professional development necessary to meet the qualification. As there is a lack of mathematics teachers generally, it is particularly hard to recruit those who are qualified to teach adult basic skills, particularly as the financial remuneration is very poor compared with compulsory-age schooling (Chanda 2005). Coben (2006) discusses the implications of this for the field. Thus, an unintended consequence of a government policy to drive up standards is that the implementation phase is being challenged by a lack of suitably qualified trainers being able to train numeracy tutors, and that not enough people want to come forward to be trained in the first place. Coupled with a general reluctance on the part of learners to do something about their mathematics, the target for improving numeracy in the adult population will be a difficult one to meet.

In 2003, a Skills for Life survey of national needs and the impact of literacy, numeracy and ICT skills was undertaken by the DfES. Over 7,800 people undertook a literacy test, and over 8,000 undertook a numeracy test, followed by over 4,600 people being interviewed. A further 4,400 people participated in an ICT test. The respondents completed a questionnaire with details about their household structure, education history, health, housing and other demographic information. On the basis of the survey, it was possible to establish the level of performance for the cohort and then extrapolate the results to the country as a whole. The results affirmed previous research by showing that nearly half of those surveyed (47 per cent) were at entry level or below for numeracy, while the figure for literacy was 16 per cent. This meant that nearly 5 million people had difficulty with literacy (defined by being at entry level or below), and a staggering 15 million had difficulty with numeracy.

The information acquired from the survey has prompted more action and policymaking, linked to an inquiry into the teaching of mathematics (Smith 2004). Recently there have been further developments including the appointment of Professor Celia Hoyles as the 'Maths Tzarina' to help identify ways of teaching mathematics effectively and encouraging more people to study it at university and then be able to teach it, thus breaking the downward spiral of poor mathematics teaching, low mathematics levels among school leavers, fewer mathematics undergraduates and fewer teachers training to teach.

NRDC has set up a Maths4Life research project to help improve the quality of teaching and learning in numeracy and non-specialist mathematics for learners in a range of post-16 provision.

Yes, but is it working?

There is no doubt that the Skills for Life strategy has had an impact on the engagement with basic skills by providers, agencies, employers and individuals. The number of people gaining a basic skills qualification is an indication that one of the measures of success has been achieved. Yet there has been resistance to many of the outcomes of the strategy by practitioners. This is hard, given that there has been so much funding, but the outcome of the strategy has been to create an infrastructure based on testing and performativity, with strong imperatives to recruit learners who must then undertake tests, within a national curriculum, to meet government targets. Perhaps more than any other aspect of Sk4L, the decision to introduce testing has been the most vociferously critiqued. The change in discourse at any basic skills practitioner gathering is an indication of how far the testing regime has permeated. People talk about a group of learners as being 'entry level two' rather than learners who want to improve their spelling! Alan Wells, the Director of the Basic Skills Agency (BSA), has also entered into the fray, arguing that the idea that a qualification in literacy is the same as a GCSE in English is a nonsense, and also that such a qualification damages the learner, who becomes identified as having a problem with literacy rather than as someone who has a qualification in being literate (Wells 2004: 3).

An interesting change in direction has been introduced over the life of the Sk4L strategy. ICT has become the 'third basic skill' and it remains to be seen whether the ambitious targets for 2007 and 2010 will be met, not by people improving their literacy and numeracy, but because they will be gaining qualifications in ICT.

There have been recent changes in agencies dealing with basic skills. ABSSU is now called the Skills for Life Strategy

Unit. The BSA holds a more critical stance about the strategy, being positioned further away from government than the directly funded strategy unit. The Standards Unit continues its work with improving quality, and following the latest general election, yet another minister has taken responsibility for life-long learning, including basic skills. It is hard to see how there can be much consistency in approach, given the ever-changing responsibility at departmental level for this important area of work.

What does Skills for Life mean for managers?

Almost anyone in FE today will be aware of the impact of the Skills for Life strategy on management. There are funds attached to attracting learners. There are obligations to develop and qualify staff. There are targets to reach. Basic skills permeates all provision, and not only do subject specialist staff need to be fully trained, but staff teaching across the range of disciplines needs to be able to identify learners who have basic skills difficulties, to offer support, and to refer them for further learning opportunities.

The formula for funding for basic skills was altered in 2002 so that literacy, language and numeracy attracted a 40 per cent higher rate than comparable courses. This higher rate of funding was intended to meet the additional costs of attracting and retaining learners who had low skills but 'high needs'. Further funding on completion of qualifications provides the normal incentive for colleges to retain their learners. All basic skills courses were free for learners, again in an attempt to provide an incentive for participation.

At the time of writing, a disastrous event for basic skills providers has resulted from the funding decisions made by the LSC. As a result of its huge success in recruiting learners in the sector, and the recent government White Papers on Skills (as noted in the previous chapter), funding for provision is centred primarily on levels one and two. Thus, non-accredited learning (levels 3 and above) and entry-level work is not being funded so generously, and there is now a real problem for providers in being able to offer learning opportunities for people at these levels.

Changes in the professional qualifications for teachers (which will be discussed in Chapters 5 and 6) will also impact on Skills for Life providers and practitioners. The situation, then, is fluid, and susceptible to changing whims of national government.

How to keep informed

Anyone who is a basic skills manager will be aware of the wealth of material available through the NRDC, the Skills for Life Strategy Unit and the Basic Skills Agency. There are, in addition, publications available through the Standards Unit and from the LSDA.

Each agency has its own publication. *Basic Skills* is the newsletter from the BSA, *Reflect* is produced by the NRDC, and the DfES has its *Update*, produced by the Skills for Life Strategy Unit.

However, to gain a critique of the effect of policy, as well as information about what is going on, two further sources are invaluable to practitioners and managers alike. The *Basic Skills Bulletin*, published by Simon Boyd, has been supplemented by the *Numeracy Bulletin* and the *Professional Development Bulletin*, demonstrating how hungry people are for information, and how important it is to keep them up to date. A long-established membership organization, Research and Practice in Adult Literacy (RaPAL), produces a journal, whose focus is not just on dissemination of information but, more important, to maintain a critique and research focus in the field. Numeracy practitioners are supported through Adults Learning Mathematics (ALM), which has annual conferences and a helpful website, as well as through the newly created Maths4Life initiative.

The financial, human resources and curricular impact, alone, of the Skills for Life strategy have had an enormous influence on college life in the last five years. The intended outcomes of the strategy should result in well-qualified teaching teams, who have tried and tested materials and resources, working towards a national curriculum, with learners who make good progress and who gain qualifications that demonstrate their learning. The reality, at the time of writing, is that many practitioners feel overwhelmed by the initiatives, providers are concerned about the impact of funding changes and compliance with professional development requirements, and learners are still finding it hard to improve their basic skills. This is an example of a difficult situation, full of tension and challenges, which has to be managed, rather than a problem than can easily be solved. The danger is that government will believe that reaching its first target of 750,000 learners improving their basic skills is an indication that all is well, and that other pressing matters can now be addressed, nudging basic skills back out of the limelight into the shadows where the field has always been.

5 A question of qualifications

'Of the three waves of policy characterizing 14–19 since 1979, the one which has had the most direct impact on the lives of young people has been curriculum change.' (Lumby and Foskett 2005: 47)

There is no one-to-one correspondence between the curriculum and qualifications, although an observer of the English education system may be forgiven for thinking so. As noted in previous chapters, the driver behind the frenetic policy arena in further education is the desire to equip people to be economically successful and to ensure the creation of an inclusive society. To achieve this requires an education system that enables young children and young adults to gain the necessary skills and knowledge to be able to enter the world of work and to live their lives successfully once they become adults. A fundamental question, then, for any education system is what purposes should it serve? Should it meet the broad needs of society; enable individuals to achieve personal development that will benefit society; enable individuals to be active participants in a democratic society; help individuals perform roles within the workforce; or help implement social change? As Lumby and Foskett (2005) argue, the English system has traditionally emphasized a humanist view, in which people would be educated for their place in society, and in which academic education was for the leaders and vocational education was for the rest. This duality has dogged the system and even now has not yet been fully exorcized.

The story begins

The starting point for analysis of the qualifications system has to take account of the kind of education system that developed from a major policy moment in 1944, the 1944 Education Act. This Act stated that all children were to be educated until they were 15 and that there were to be three forms of secondary education: academic education provided by grammar schools, general education provided by secondary modern schools and vocational education provided by technical schools. The tripartite system was meant to reflect the abilities of the population. The Act set in stone the notion that some people can think, and others can do. It also reflected the notion of meritocracy whereby young people who were able to think would be able to earn their place in academic grammar schools through their own efforts, rather than through privilege.

At the same time, the original aims of further education – ensuring that young people and adults could train for their chosen vocation – further reinforced the idea that those who could 'do' had appropriate provision to help them do so effectively. For those who could think, the universities were there to ensure that they would finish their education and enter the world of management, leadership and the professions.

Within this system, there needed to be a way to demonstrate that people had indeed learnt the knowledge and skills they were intended to achieve. It is here that the qualifications story begins.

Twenty-five years ago, there were General Certificates of Education at Ordinary Level (GCE O levels), which were gained in a variety of subjects studied at secondary school through public examinations. These O levels were aimed at the top 20 per cent of the ability range. A Certificate of Secondary Education (CSE) existed for the next 40 per cent of pupils. By the time young people ended the compulsory stage of education (which was by now 16 years of age), 10 per cent of the population were able to study for a Certificate at Advanced Level (GCE A level), usually in the sixth form of a grammar school, but also at further education colleges. Only through achievement at A level could young people progress to higher education at universities. The system, then, could 'sort' young people into groups according to their apparent academic ability, and the way to do so was through a public examination system.

However, even 25 years ago, it was apparent that the system was leading to large numbers of people leaving school without any formal qualifications at all and that the type of qualification and the way it was achieved through certain kinds of assessment, notably public examinations, did not demonstrate what many young people had actually achieved during their 12 years of compulsory schooling.

The answer to this problem was to introduce in 1985 a different kind of qualification, the General Certificate of Secondary Education, GCSE, which had a grade system of A to G, intended to show that, even at the lower grades, people could gain a qualification. The unintended consequence of this decision has been that only grades A★ to C are deemed to be worthwhile and a 'Grade C cliff' (Cockett and Callaghan 1996) has developed, which persists as a selection device for further education, training and employment. Looking back to 1979, there is little difference between people with O levels and those who have gained five GCSE A★–C passes and between those with CSEs and those with passes at other grades, leading Lumby and Foskett to conclude that 'despite a quarter century of changes, the fundamental structure and nature of the 14–16 curriculum remains the same' (2005: 51).

Meanwhile, what has happened to those who did not gain O levels or GCSE grades A★–C? As noted in Chapter 2, rising youth unemployment in the late 1970s and throughout the 1980s led to a number of training schemes, including the Youth Opportunities Scheme (YOS), which ran between 1978 and 1983, and the Youth Training Scheme (YTS), which ran from 1983 to 1989. At the same time, the White Paper *A New Training Initiative* (1981) led to the creation of the National Vocational Qualifications System, with the formation of the National Council for Vocational Qualifications (NCVQ) in 1986, and the creation of National Vocational Qualifications (NVQs). This qualifications system was fundamentally different from the academic GCSE and A level format. In this system competences were assessed against a set of industry standards which had been translated into an amazingly complex array of assessment criteria, range statements and stipulated assessment methods. The system did not require a curriculum as such and certainly did not specify time spent learning or acquiring skills. It was based on outputs, not inputs.

Working with the unqualified

The consequence of this vocational qualifications system was that young people who were still at school, or in further education colleges, were not yet in the workplace, and could not, therefore, demonstrate their knowledge and skills based on industry standards, since they had not yet gained much experience of performing the tasks required. The solution to *this* problem was the creation of a more generic vocational qualification, the General National Vocational Qualification, GNVQ, advocated in the 1991 White Paper, *Education and Training for the 21st Century* (DES/DE 1991). Now there were key vocational areas, such as health and social care, leisure and tourism, which help individuals not only to develop some occupational knowledge and understanding, but also to demonstrate core skills of communication, application of number and information technology. These core skills eventually became key skills, and included, in addition to the first three domains, working in teams, problem-solving and personal skills.

During the 1980s and 1990s, when vocational qualifications were being developed for adults and young people, there were attempts to change the concentration on a primarily academic curriculum in schools and the accompanying qualifications system of GCSEs and A levels. The use of key skills was advocated in academic qualifications, and was even proselytized in higher education. However, nowhere was there a commitment to their adoption, and despite the creation of specific qualifications in the key skills, there was no agreement on their integration into the curriculum, the qualifications system or the ways in which they would be used by employers (noted by Hodgson and Spours (2002) as 'half-hearted'). Various attempts to influence the curriculum to take account of business and industry needs had been undertaken, including the use of the Technical and Vocational Education Initiative (TVEI) in 1985, in which young people were encouraged to study vocational subjects as part of their GCSEs. Once again, these subjects were increasingly seen as being suitable for people with less academic ability, and the vocational/academic divide was further reinforced.

While the policymakers continued to grapple with vocational qualifications, introducing Modern Apprenticeships (MAs) in 1995 and organizing the infrastructure to support employment training through the creation of Training and Enterprise Councils (TECs), one area of the qualifications system, the A level, remained unchallengeable. Its use as a gatekeeper to higher education, further education and employment ensured that it earned the name of the 'gold standard'. Yet by the end of the 1990s it was clear that the original design for the top 10 per cent of young people was unworkable in a system of GCSEs and NVQs and for a population of young people who were now staying on in the education system for much longer than their parents had.

Meanwhile, adult learners needed a qualifications system that was accessible to them in terms of time and content. In the 1980s, a new, alternative qualifications system was developed through the National Open College Network (NOCN). This was originally set up to help create a means to accredit the learning that was taking place in adult and community centres. It aimed to help adults who had returned to learning in informal programmes gain credit for their study and thereby enable them to move into the more formal, accredited systems of further and higher education. This alternative route continues today to offer learners the opportunity to accumulate credit through small 'chunks' of learning, and the system also enables providers to identify learning outcomes which match their own curriculum, rather than having to meet the national curriculum in schools (FEU 1995; Hodgson and Spours 1997; and see www.nocn.org.uk).

Tinkering with A levels

By 2000, the English post-compulsory system comprised a 'triple track' system with training, vocational qualifications including NVQs, GNVQs and MAs, and academic qualifications, A levels. All of these qualifications were available in FE colleges, but the systematic divide of academic versus vocational qualifications persisted. More young people took A levels in their school sixth forms or at sixth-form colleges and most vocational qualifications were taken in further education colleges. Yet for years there had been calls to create a unitary system, which would not perpetuate the academic/vocational divide, and one way to achieve this was to develop a British baccalaureate (FEU 1983; Hodgson and Spours 1997; Hodgson 2000). In 1997 the DfEE's consultation paper *Qualifying for Success* identified the need to restructure the qualifications system, and the resultant Curriculum 2000 was intended to achieve this by creating Advanced Certificates in Vocational Education (ACVEs) to replace GNVQs and modularizing the A level system further, so that there were Advanced Subsidiary examinations (AS) and A2 examinations, which could together lead to A levels. The mix and match system proved to be a bureaucratic nightmare for the awarding bodies, and the AS examinations highly burdensome on an already pressured cohort of young people. In the summer of 2002 controversies about marking standards led to the resignation of the then director of the Qualifications and Curriculum Authority, Sir William Stubbs, and the Minister of State for Education, Estelle Morris. It was clear that a thorough review of the whole system for 14–19-year-olds was needed and Mike Tomlinson was asked to undertake this increasingly troublesome task.

The Tomlinson Review

What were the problems that Tomlinson was asked to address? First was the divide between academic and vocational pathways for 14–19-year-olds.

Second was the underpinning divide between middle-class people, who generally do well in the academic education system, and working-class people, who in the past have tended to inhabit the vocational part of the education system. This divide has changed, of course, in real terms over the past 30 years, but there is still evidence that people from families who have benefited from the academic education system tend to have children who also benefit and that people who are least qualified tend to have children who also do not gain as many qualifications as their more middle-class peers. Given that qualifications are used as a selection device to such a great extent, the consequences for individuals are enormous (Fine-gold and Soskice 1988). Estimates that people with degrees, for example, will earn thousands of pounds more than their less qualified counterparts have even been used by the current government to encourage young people to progress to higher education.

Further evidence that young people do not tend to move out of their 'track' (Hodkinson *et al*. 1996; Bloomer 1997) reveals that those who have chosen a vocational pathway or possibly have not even taken part in any further education and training once they officially left school are still unlikely to change paths, even if their circumstances change, or they simply develop later than their peers. Coupled with this is the 'curse' of class, so that any new idea to help the lowest achievers merely reinforces their position, as the creation of qualifications for basic skills testifies.

The position is not helped by the fact that the qualifications system is a jungle within which young people get lost trying to make sense of the courses and qualifications available to them (DfES 2003). How, then, can a review of the system help move towards a framework that is more equitable and fit for its purpose?

Tomlinson's deliberations

Tomlinson was asked to address the following issues:

- motivating learning – overcoming disengagement by young learners
- developing knowledge, skills and attributes for the future
- improving the quality of learning

- promoting 'effective' learner choice
- promoting progression
- developing stronger vocational education and better employer engagement.

Tomlinson noted that one of the problems for young people is that they have so many external examinations. Taking an average eight GCSEs and three A levels meant losing about two terms' worth of learning in preparation and exam time. He noted the:

> 'excessive burdens on learners, teachers, institutions and awarding bodies from the number of examinations which many young people now take, the increasing number of examination entries and the administrative and other arrangements which support the examinations system.' (Tomlinson 2004: 58)

Tomlinson's response to these challenges was to propose a brave and bold overhaul of the qualifications system for 14–19-year-olds. He advocated a multi-level system of diplomas at four levels: entry, foundation, intermediate and advanced. There would be 'lines' within the diplomas rather than the current vocational/academic divide. There would be holistic programmes of learning which would be recognized by the award of diplomas. Within any programme of learning, there would be a common core, including a personalized learning project. Apprenticeships would be linked with work-based learning. There would be assessment for learning as opposed to assessment of learning. Teachers and lecturers would be responsible for the assessment of learning, as would the awarding bodies, who would continue their role with public examinations. There would also be within the core a focus on functional English and mathematics. This was to be a long-term reform involving all the stakeholders.

What actually happened to the proposals?

It is important to remember that by the time Tomlinson had completed his report, the government was about to begin preparations for a general election. As with much government policy work, certain decisions were put 'on hold' during the run up to the election. However, in the case of Tomlinson, Government rejected the bold proposal to create diplomas instead of the GCSE and A level system. Instead, it proposed to keep the latter, but to develop a new general diploma for those gaining five A*–C GCSEs. There would be new vocational diplomas in subjects such as healthcare, engineering and hairdressing from 2008. The volume of coursework for GCSEs would be cut. A levels would be strengthened to include options to stretch the most able pupils, and there are even discussions about using HE-level modules within schools to achieve this.

Tomlinson had been set five tests: to stretch the most able young people, to address the historic failure to provide high-quality vocational learning to motivate young people, to prepare young people for the world of work, to stop the high drop-out rate at 16 and 18, and to reduce the burden of assessment. The Secretary of State for Education, Ruth Kelly, justified the rejection of Tomlinson's radical proposals by arguing:

> 'We will not transform opportunities by abolishing what is good, what works and what is recognized by employers, universities, pupils and parents. We must build on what is good in the system and reform and replace what is not working.' (*Education and Training Parliamentary Monitor*, March 2005: 3)

Kelly proposed that there would be a new programme for 14–16-year-olds, which would allow learning at work, and for the high achievers there would be a report of unit grades from A levels to enable universities to distinguish better between applicants for over-subscribed places. The result, then, was an acceptance of the problems outlined by Tomlinson, but a bolt-on rather than radical change to the system. There will now be not one diploma but 15, and those working with 14–19 learners will once again be involved in the delivery of these awards. As for the fundamental problem that this chapter started with, what has happened to the academic/vocational divide? As David Bell, HMI Chief Inspector noted:

'Continuing with the current GCSE and A Level structure carries the risk of continuing the historic divide between academic and vocational courses, which has ill-served too many young people in the past.' (*Education and Training Parliamentary Monitor*, March 2005: 4)

Framework for Achievement (FfA)

While Tomlinson was working on 14–19 developments, the QCA, the LSC and awarding bodies were involved in examining a new framework for learning for adults, the Framework for Achievement (FfA). As with Tomlinson, the underlying principle behind the Framework for Achievement was to enable transfer and progression but this time for adults, who will have a range of needs. Tomlinson recognized the need to have a common format for credit across the 14–19 and adult frameworks and that young people should be able to draw down units from the adult framework that they could later use towards qualifications as adults.

In the Framework consultation, the proposals set out a 'radical new structure that recognizes achievement through a system of interconnected units' (QCA 2004: 2). It was designed to help employees gain credit from in-house training, for example, and for private training providers to offer short courses, which would also become accredited. The system would have outcomes related to employment sectors and would be driven by the needs of employers.

There would be a common bank of units, which would contribute to one or more qualifications. Existing systems such as that of the National Open College Network would be recognized.

Why develop a new framework? Well, the current qualifications system is not inclusive enough, not responsive enough and certainly too complicated and bureaucratic. Yet there is a vast experience of unitised qualifications in the awarding bodies' system. Setting up a national qualifications framework would facilitate the provision of opportunities for adult learners to gain credit within the system that would be recognized by employers, further and higher education institutions and professional bodies. The proposed framework would work in parallel with the Scottish Credit and Qualifications Framework (SCQF), the Credit and Qualifications Framework for Wales (CQFW) and the Northern Ireland Credit Accumulation and Transfer Scheme (NICATS).

The specific proposals are to:

- create a standard template for all units
- support collaboration between different users of the framework in developing units and qualifications
- rationalize unit development through the establishment of a unit databank
- use credit value to indicate the relative size of achievements
- develop a credit transcript in which all individual achievements will be recognized
- establish a standard format for all qualifications titles.

With the use of information technology, the standard template for units, for example, can be achieved by creating a unit databank: an electronic template that can be stored and transferred between all users. The initial resource implications for awarding bodies and users in colleges and training provider centres are huge, but ultimately would help create a level of information interchange that would ensure that learners can be tracked throughout their learning careers. The resulting data created will enable monitoring of policy initiatives to be both systematic and efficient.

The FfA may have been established by the time this book is published, so readers may already be working within the implementation phase. By 2010 all qualifications for adults will be accredited within the FfA.

What does this mean in terms of policy analysis?

During the past 30 years, there has been rapid change following a comparatively stable policy space, usually as a response to necessity. As far as the qualifications system was concerned, the use of O and A levels enjoyed over 40 years of relative stability from 1944 to 1986, notwithstanding some changes to the system. After this, as a response to youth unemployment, and economic problems, there have been a number of what Dass and Parker (1999) call 'episodes', which usually occur at the end of an economic crisis and which are attempts to prevent any further crisis. These episodes require considerable change to the education system, and are therefore systemic in nature.

Despite the current rhetoric of creating a system which is demand-led, the reality, of course, is that the system has been continually tinkered with on the supply side. The qualifications framework is a testament to this tinkering. Rather than meeting the needs of the learners, the framework remains dense, confusing and even damaging, particularly when young people are forced to compete for places at some universities, having gained four or more A grade A levels, and are at the same time reading that there has been a 'dumbing down' of their qualifications in the media because so many are successful in gaining good grades. More worryingly, for those who do not engage with any form of learning, euphemistically described as those 'not in education, employment and training' (NEET), the focus on gaining qualifications further excludes them, as a survey of vocational qualifications on behalf of the Learning and Skills Research Centre identified:

> 'Issues of structure and implementation seem to be placed on a back-burner while the government focuses on targets and accountability. Ironically, perhaps, this review suggests that excessive focus on qualifications may be especially counter-productive for hard-to-reach learners.' (Stasz *et al.* 2004: 64)

Ainley (2003) has noted that the learning policies of the past years have actually contributed to the way in which many learners are 'clambering up the down escalator of depreciating credentials' (Ainley 2003: 405), further exacerbated by a rough divide between people who have 'respectable' qualifications and those who have become an underclass, and who are becoming 'intergenerationally immobile' (Roberts 2001: 115).

Wider education policy

Tomlinson has not occurred in a vacuum. There are three wider policy aspects that are relevant. The first concerns the

Five Year Strategy, released in July 2004, which is the government's education manifesto to 2008. There are targets within this strategy, for example that 60 per cent of young people should gain five good GCSEs, and that 180,000 14–16-year-olds should take vocational subjects. At the same time, the government is intending to expand its academies, sixth forms and specialist schools, somewhat going against the spirit of Tomlinson's proposals to create a coherent, collaborative model.

The second is the Skills Strategy, with its long evolutionary period of change, as discussed in Chapter 2.

Finally, there are Public Service Agreements (PSAs) with targets, for example, performance at 16 and 19 years, working with the 'disengaged' and entry into HE. One target, for example, is that by 2010, 90 per cent of young people will by age 22 have participated in a full-time programme fitting them for entry into higher education or skilled employment.

What are the consequences of education policies that abound with targets? An annual curriculum report for 2003/4 provides a snapshot of activity, demonstrating just how much external testing young people have been subjected to:

> There were 5.3 million GCSE results, 0.7 million A level results, nearly 1 million AS exam results, 42,000 VCE results. Of the GCSEs, there were 110,000 vocational subjects taken. There are over 100 awarding bodies issuing a million certificates in these vocational subjects every year. Every year 2 million children are tested for key stages in schools in England. No wonder the performativity culture drives future policy making! (Besley, 2005d)

Besley has identified that there are no less than seven Education Acts, four White Papers, two Green Papers and three Tomlinson Reports addressing vocational learning for 14–19-year-olds (Besley 2005d) and if qualifications and skills are included, there are also the Skills Strategy, the Framework for Achievement and the Foster and Leitch Reviews. Yet still there is no clear indication that any significant change to A levels or GCSEs will occur as a result of the intended review of qualifications in 2008. The state of uncertainty, then, remains for all providers of 14–19 education. As Ken Boston, CEO of the QCA noted, 'ultimately, the demand side, learners, industry, universities, parents and teachers will determine whether A levels remain or not' (Besley 2005d). Kelly perhaps summed up the situation when she discussed how aspects of Tomlinson were being taken forward, by arguing that 'there will be radical change but also a key point of stability' by retaining A levels and GCSEs but introducing Diplomas, and also concentrating on ways to attract disengaged learners, to stretch more able ones, and to ensure that standards in literacy and numeracy are improved so that no one will gain a GCSE without having a functional level of literacy and numeracy.

The policy agenda is not limited to England. Much further afield in Europe, the Lisbon Strategy (March 2000) identified as its goal that by 2010 the EU would become the 'most competitive and dynamic knowledge-based economy in the world, capable of sustainable economic growth with more and better jobs and greater social cohesion' (EU 2000b). Note how, once again, the two goals of economic success and social cohesion are fundamental components of the strategy. The EU strategy is not one of compliance but of advocacy, attempting to encourage, for example, educational institutions to work more effectively with business, helping to foster the skills of the EU workforce, facilitating the mobility of students and teachers and paying particular attention to the problems of unemployed young people. These aims fit closely with those identified by the government in England and the rest of the UK.

What does this mean for managers?

First, the qualifications framework continues to shift so much that managers, particularly curriculum managers, need to keep informed about changes by working closely with the awarding bodies. Today most awarding bodies have policy analysts who can disseminate their understanding of policy affecting the qualifications framework to their centres. This is an important source of information for any manager in the sector.

Second, planning provision has to take account of the uncertain terrain. In addition, on a pragmatic basis, learners who are coming through the doors today need to be given assurances that the qualifications for which they want to study are available and, more important, have credibility. This requires up-to-date advice and guidance systems, so that any provider can enable learners to make appropriate decisions for their careers.

There are implications for managers adapting to new qualifications frameworks. Managers who were involved in the sector in the 1990s will remember the need to accredit staff who assessed NVQs. The staff development resources, as well as time resources, required were immense, and any new initiative, such as the proposed introduction of a suite of Diplomas, requires consideration of the human resources, as well as the bureaucratic resources, to support the changes.

As the implementation of the 14–19-year-old strategy is a ten-year programme, managers reading this book should be kept busy for some time to come! Perhaps the last word should rest with Stasz and Wright:

> 'There is presently a high level of interest in creating a system that works for the UK, and also a high level of frustration and sense of déjà vu among academics, policy-makers and practitioners who have been involved in the vocational learning enterprise. The alternatives seem to be to continue "tinkering", possibly ineffectively, with the current system or to adopt more radical reform, possibly of a sort that involves more regulation and stronger leadership ... there is still a strong debate as to what a vocational learning system for the twenty-first century should look like. The current policy directives may help to clarify that vision, provided that outstanding concerns and issues are not ignored and current initiatives are given time to take hold and are properly evaluated.' (Stasz and Wright 2004: 38)

6 Assuring quality

'Independent inspection has played an important role in driving up public service standards.' (DfES, 2005a: 2.1.5)

The quest for quality is unceasing and relentless in the learning and skills sector. Any manager reading this book will be only too familiar with the inspection regimes that have been adopted by the Learning and Skills Council (LSC), the awarding bodies, the Adult Learning Inspectorate (ALI) and the Office for Standards in Education (Ofsted), along with managers' own internal institutional quality assurance procedures. It is no wonder that many staff are cynical about attempts to reduce bureaucracy in the system, when they are so overwhelmed by completing forms to demonstrate that they have undertaken their audits, monitored outputs and identified areas of good practice as well as followed up on issues for development and change!

How did this situation arise? In educational terms, before incorporation in 1992/3, the further education colleges were part of a well-established inspection regime which had been operating for nearly a century. The idea that any educational provision should be inspected was definitely not a new idea of the Conservative government in the 1980s. The process was at that time already operating through Her Majesty's Inspectorate (HMI), and inspectors were appointed who were specialists in primary, secondary or further and adult education, as well as those with specific responsibility for subject disciplines. As further education colleges were part of LEAs, they were inspected through the HMI system. In addition, each LEA had its own advisory service, in which there were specialists in parallel with the HMI system. Within the LEA advisory services, advisors took a more developmental approach, but helped to assure the quality of the educational provision, as they were acquainted with staff on a more personal level, and were able to disseminate good practice and help staff address challenges and difficulties they encountered.

Once the further education colleges were taken out of LEA control, a new form of inspection was created by the Further Education Funding Council (FEFC), and once again, this decision profoundly changed the way in which colleges were inspected. It must be remembered that, at the same time, schools were being monitored more closely, as government took more central control over their affairs. The 1988 Education Reform Act was responsible for many of these changes, as noted in Chapter 2.

A further influence on the changing inspection regime was the idea that accountability could be partially achieved through the publication of inspection findings. Originally, HMI reports could be complimentary or critical, but they were confidential (Burgess 1964). In fact, in the 1960s staff did not see the reports and, as Burgess noted, 'the inspectors do not give orders either to teachers or to the local authorities. Their job is to inspect, to praise or blame, and to advise. It is the job of those in charge . . . to do whatever is necessary' (1964: 46).

This situation had changed dramatically by the 1990s. At this time school performance league tables were being created, and the FEFC decided that its inspection regime would be open to public scrutiny through the publication of its reports. At the same time, the use of the web was increasing, and it was possible for inspection reports to be made available electronically. These original reports are still available from the FEFC archive, and make interesting reading in terms of the changing nature of what was inspected and how it was reported, in light of the current inspection framework.

Who is now responsible for quality?

Most colleges now have quality assurance managers to ensure that they meet both the LSC inspection requirements and awarding body criteria. Colleges today tend to have 'flat' structures, with full-time members of staff often responsible for large areas of the curriculum. There has been a casualization of staff, so that more teaching staff are now employed on temporary and/or part-time contracts. Evidence provided to the Education and Employment Committee of the House of Commons (Select Committee) by the National Association of Teachers in Further and Higher Education (NATFHE) in 1997 suggested that more than 42 per cent of staff employed for more than 15 hours per week were working on temporary contracts (vol. 2, appendix 53, para. 43), so there was an increasing reliance on temporary staff to deliver large parts of the curriculum. Such staff often held responsibility for whole programmes. This, linked with loss of staff through early retirement and voluntary redundancy, has created a sector with a small core of full-time and fractional staff and a significant proportion of hourly paid and agency staff (Bailey and Ainley 2000: 45; Hillier and Jameson 2004).

There is an assumption throughout the quality assurance system that having too many part-time staff is bad for quality. While it is the case that hourly paid staff have fewer opportunities to engage in professional development or participate in quality-raising initiatives, not least because they may simply be working elsewhere or have other domestic responsibilities, they are not necessarily providing poorer-quality sessions to their learners (Hillier and Jameson 2004). However one of the ongoing demands for management in any LSC funded provision is to ensure that all staff are given the appropriate resources to provide learning of the highest quality. This is not easy if a high proportion of the staff only come to the institution for a few hours a week.

A common approach to assuring quality?

Now that the LSC funds learning that was hitherto funded as Schedule 2 provision by the FEFC, as well as all 'other learning' (that is, non-accredited adult education and all work-based training), it has needed to ensure that the quality of its provision extends across the range of learning opportunities for which it is responsible. The inspection of this provision is shared between two inspectorates: Ofsted deals with provision for those under 19 and the Adult Learning Inspectorate (ALI) with all provision for adults. Both inspectorates agreed a common inspection framework to help provide coherence and consistency in the sector. ALI created Excalibur in 2004, which is a database containing examples of college good practice. The model of inspection is moving from the 'snapshot' approach towards a more longitudinal approach with a number of small-scale visits. A scheme has also been launched for inspecting employers offering workplace training. In September 2004, the armed services requested inspection by ALI for the vast amount of training they undertake, particularly with young recruits.

The common inspection framework has as its core the question, 'How effective and efficient is the provision of education and training in meeting the needs of learners, and why?' (ALI/Ofsted 2001: 3).

This question is answered by evaluating and reporting on the following aspects of provision.

- What is achieved: the standards reached and learners' achievements, taking account of their prior attainment and intended learning goals.
- The quality of teaching, training, assessment and learning.
- Other aspects of provision that contribute to the standards achieved, such as the range, planning and content of courses or programmes; resources; and support for individual learners.
- The effectiveness with which the provision is managed, is quality assured and improved, and how efficiently resources are used to ensure that the provision gives value for money.
- The extent to which provision is educationally and socially inclusive, and promotes equality of access to education and training, including provision for learners with learning difficulties or disabilities. (Ibid.)

There is currently a new format for inspection, Cycle 2, which works with providers' own quality improvement agenda, in which inspectors have more discretion over what they inspect following the institution's self-analysis. This aims to foster a long-term relationship between the inspectorate and the institution which should lead to a development-orientated and quality-enhancing approach. Colleges that have previously gained grades one and two will have fewer inspection days than those with lower grades. The notice to inspect will be shortened, thereby reducing the temptation to produce mounds of paper for evidence to the inspectors. In 2005 a revised Common Inspection Framework was published to take account of the changing 'lighter touch' system (ALI/Ofsted 2005).

The major challenge of trying to create an inspection framework that can deal with further and adult education, work-based training and 14–19 provision is that it is difficult to cover such a diverse pattern of learning provision in one common framework. There are over 400 colleges and 1,200 work-based learning providers to be inspected on a four-year cycle, and 30 prisons to be inspected annually. In July 2005, the DfES launched a consultation on dealing with the more specialized forms of adult education and employer training, with a view to rationalizing the inspection system. 'These plans form one of the key strands in the government's strategy to reform public service inspection to focus more closely on the need of users' (Kelly 2005, reported in Besley 2005d).

The proposal is to bring ALI and Ofsted together, to reduce bureaucracy, create flexibility and focus on the needs of users. The need to monitor 14–19 activity is a 'powerful' driver for this proposal, but as ALI's journal *Talisman* shows, it has undertaken an enormous amount of work in the past four years, with over 3,345 inspections, claims of £6 million efficiency savings, and as a government agency, it has even won plaudits for its work, including Best Government Information Publication for its Annual Report in 2003. Its Excalibur website is popular, with nearly 700 hits daily, and it is important that any change does not lose such a successful facility for managers in the sector.

The DfES consultation draws on a Policy on Inspection of Public Services (OPSR, 2003), which defined the characteristics of the inspection of public services as being: independent of service providers; providing assurance about the safe and proper delivery of the services; contributing to improvement of the services; reporting in public; and delivering value for money. The report identified a number of 'expectations', which were defined within ten principles of inspection:

- Purpose of improvement: inspectors should have an explicit concern to contribute to the improvement of the service.
- Focus on outcomes: considering the end users rather than internal management arrangements.
- User perspective: inspections should have a clear focus on the experience of the users, and should also encourage innovation and diversity and not be solely compliance-based.
- Proportionate to risk: good performers should not have to undergo as much inspection, so that resources are concentrated on areas of greatest risk.
- Self-assessment: inspectors should encourage rigorous self-assessment and take these assessments into account.
- Impartial evidence: qualitative and quantitative evidence should be validated and credible.
- Criteria: inspectors should be explicit about the criteria they use to form judgements.
- Openness: inspectors should be open about their processes and be willing to take complaints seriously.
- Value for money: the process of inspection itself should be cost-effective.
- Learning from experience: inspectors should assess their own impact on the service provider's ability to improve and share best practice.

This policy is an interesting development from the original HMI format. Now, the value of an inspection is being called to account, and the excesses of the FEFC and Ofsted inspection regimes, in which mountains of paper were produced in 'base rooms' for inspectors' examination, and thousands of managers and lecturers underwent sleepless nights, may become a distant bad memory.

The new 'light touch' regime also signals a change in approach, so that areas of greatest need are given most attention. The policy is expected to work within other government policy objectives, including the two White Papers, *Skills: Getting on in Business, Getting on at Work* (DfES 2005b) and *14– 19 Education and Skills* (DfES 2005c). The reform is aligned to the Chancellor's announcement in March 2005 that eleven government inspectorates would be reduced to four, so that there would be single inspectorates for justice and community safety; for education and children's services; for adult social care and health; and for local services. His proposal would begin to rationalize the inspectorates,

> 'in order to simplify and manage better the complex pattern of multiple scrutiny that service providers experience and reduce the amount of inspection activity and burden generated, and the variety of approaches that is a feature of having many bodies performing similar tasks.' (Brown 2005)

Interestingly, although the proposed merger is to take place in April 2007, the DfES has announced that after the consultation period, which ended in November 2005, 'there is unlikely to be an opportunity for further consultation' between the final decision and legislation.

A national quality improvement body

Who represents the quality assurance interests of the sector in a developmental way, rather than through an inspection regime? Before incorporation, the Further Education Unit (FEU) had a role in undertaking research and development with staff in the sector, as a way of creating innovative methods to foster learning and disseminating good practice. There was a staff college, the Further Education Staff College (FESC) at Blagdon, which ran short residential programmes for managers and lecturers in further and adult education. In 1995, the FEU became the Further Education Development Agency (FEDA). Its role was to continue the work of FEU with a stronger focus on development.

Once the Learning and Skills Act had been passed, FEDA changed its name to the Learning and Skills Development Agency (LSDA). It continued its role in fostering good practice through research and development, but it also launched its Learning and Skills Research Centre in 2000, which could

commission research as well as work closely wit
managers at LSDA.

A consultation on the role of LSDA resulted in re
'welcoming clear statements on who was responsible for what
aspect of quality improvement in the sector'. Given that this
appears currently to reside with the DfES, the Learning and
Skills Council (LSC), Jobcentre Plus, LLUK and the Centre for
Excellence in Leadership, it will be interesting to see how the
answer, which is 'primary responsibility for improving the
quality of provision rests with the provider', can be helped by
the creation of a 'single point of reference' with a 'single voice'
setting out clear standards, expectations and good practice.

The Quality Improvement Agency (QIA), established in
2006, is expected to simplify and bring coherence to quality
improvement in the sector. It has a strategic role setting priorities and commissioning improvement services and materials,
which it will also quality assure. The Excalibur model of ALI is
expected to be utilized by the new QIA, particularly once the
extended Ofsted is established, so that the dissemination of
good practice continues.

The DfES set out its five-year strategy for quality improvement in post-compulsory education in 2003. By 2008 the
learning and skills sector would:

- be fully responsive to the needs of learners and employers
- attract strong and effective staff and leaders
- identify and meet its own priorities and targets for
  improvement, drawing effectively on the findings of
  inspection and annual self-assessment. (DfES 2004: 4)

The LSC has a primary role for ensuring quality. The council
achieves this through its business cycle of planning, target setting and reviewing performance against success measures. The
two inspectorates have evolved to place emphasis on
improvement and self-improvement by providers. The DfES
maintains that managing change and improving quality lies 'first
and foremost with providers' (ibid.), which affirms Burgess's
claim back in 1964. However, the DfES has argued that there is
still too much mediocre provision, and that quality improvement must be accelerated to achieve the Success for All reforms.

The purpose of the QIA is to focus on strategic quality improvement, which will 'encourage everyone working in the sector to be advocates for continuous improvement, leading to increased responsiveness, excellent learning opportunities for all and a sector which delivers to all parts of society' (ibid.).

How will this be achieved? By providing access for all providers to a single authoritative source of advice which will help them in their three-year development plans. The QIA will act as a broker to help those providers who have failed to meet their targets, or who have been identified through inspection as being a cause for concern, to undertake a programme of tailored improvement activities. It is expected that the QIA will champion excellence and celebrate success, thereby acting as a catalyst for change. There will be opportunities for the QIA to pilot, test and evaluate improvement approaches. By commissioning materials and services, it will maintain a certain distance from the work of the DfES and the inspectorate, thereby providing a certain level of objectivity in this sensitive area.

The three priorities for QIA's first years of operation will be to develop a coherent national approach to quality improvement, to work with providers and to develop the work programme.

Joined-up enhancement: the role of staff in the sector

It is clear that the role of the QIA will be to work with existing organizations, which in turn have been created as part of the government agenda for improvement. One key component of any improvement strategy is the staff who have to implement change and also develop their own professional knowledge and skill to ensure that the learning opportunities for which they are responsible are of good quality.

How, then, has the quality enhancement of staff in the sector been managed?

First, let us examine the professional development of staff. If we look back to the 1970s, there were at that stage very few professional development opportunities for staff in further education. There was a qualification, the City and Guilds

Teaching Certificate, the 730, which people could take, but there was no requirement to do so. Many instructors and lecturers joined the sector with their own professional qualifications or with industry experience, but they were certainly not qualified to teach. Over the next 30 years, it became increasingly apparent that staff should be encouraged to gain teaching qualifications. The awarding bodies created a variety of pathways, which were either generic, such as the City and Guilds 730 series, or specialist, such as the Royal Society of Arts (RSA) qualifications in teaching dance or typing.

As noted in Chapter 5, the qualifications framework became outcomes-based from the 1980s onwards, and professional qualifications for staff reflected this change. FEFC inspection reports commented on the number of qualified teaching staff and linked this to indicators of teaching quality. The further education sector was increasingly criticized for the quality of its learning provision. This eventually led to the idea that there should, as with other industries, be a national training organization (NTO) responsible for the quality of standards in the FE sector. As a result, the Further Education National Training Organisation, FENTO, was created in 1999.

FENTO's key aim was to provide high-quality teaching, to create effective opportunities for learning and to enable all learners to achieve to the best of their ability. FENTO developed a set of standards, in consultation with the sector, which have been incorporated into the following key areas:

1. assessing learners' needs
2. planning and preparing teaching and learning programmes for groups and individuals
3. developing and using a range of teaching and learning techniques
4. managing the learning process
5. providing learners with support
6. assessing the outcomes of learning and learners' achievements
7. reflecting on and evaluating one's own performance and planning future practice
8. meeting professional requirements.

The standards are benchmarked against three stages of teaching/ training qualifications: Introductory (equivalent to City and Guilds 7307 Teachers' Certificate Part One), Intermediate (equivalent to City and Guilds Teachers' Certificate or Year One of the Certificate in Education) and Certificated (equivalent to the Certificate in Education or PGCE). FENTO subsequently developed a set of teaching standards for basic skills, as noted in Chapter 4, for literacy, numeracy and ESOL. It became a requirement in 2001 that all staff new to teaching in the sector must gain an initial teaching qualification.

Once again, the policy for working with staff in the FE sector has had to take account of the wider economic policies of the day. When the government decided to change the system of national training organizations into one of sector skills councils, it was decided that FENTO, along with the NTOs for adult and community learning (PAULO) and employment training (ENTO), would become incorporated into the Lifelong Learning Sector Skills Council, LLUK, in 2004.

At the time of writing, the FENTO standards are still being used for initial teacher training and professional development, but these are subject to review, pending the creation of a new teacher training framework announced in 2004. The new proposals have been developed partly as a response to the changing learner profile. Now that 14–16-year-olds are being taught within FE, staff who have no qualification to teach young people in the compulsory system are finding themselves working with school-age children. There is also a difference in conditions of service for staff in FE compared with their school counterparts, as school teachers enjoy longer holidays and higher pay. Those who have qualified teacher status (QTS) are increasingly tempted to move back into school teaching, and those without this status are finding themselves working with young people who have been hard to teach in schools! However, the thrust of the new proposals is to enable people who work in post-compulsory education to gain a teaching qualification that will license them to practice. There will be a 'passport' to teach, which can be gained over 30 guided learning hours of professional development, much like the original introductory level of the FENTO approved qualifications. This will be followed by full training, which new teachers can take up to five years to complete. The full award will be Qualified Teacher Learning and Skills (QTLS) status. People beginning the training for the passport will be registered with the Institute for Learning (IfL) and, once qualified, will have the threshold licence to practise. Once the full QTLS is gained, they will hold a full licence to practise. This licence will need to be renewed by completing an annual tariff of continuing professional development (CPD).

Building on the model for COVEs (Centres of Vocational Excellence), Centres for Excellence in Teacher Training will be created. The FENTO standards, despite their important role in standardizing ITT in the past five years, do not yet cover the wide range of contexts in the learning and skills sector. The LLUK is therefore charged with developing the standards by spring 2006.

Another focus for improving the quality of the sector through workforce development is in the area of management and leadership. To help develop the skills and knowledge of people responsible for the learning and skills sector at senior management levels, a Centre for Excellence in Leadership (CEL) was created in 2003. As noted in Chapter 3, its remit is to enable those responsible at strategic levels to meet the demands of an effective and efficient sector through the management of individual institutions.

CEL aims to do this by providing a Careers Development Service; by coaching, mentoring and work shadowing; as well as via more traditional programmes of professional development.

Policy analysis of quality

What does the story of quality assurance in the sector tell us about how policy has been created and enacted? We have to look back, in policy terms, to previous Conservative governments that had, in turn, been influenced by ideas of individual responsibility and accountability stemming from neo-liberal views on how public services should be funded and managed. Neo-liberal promotion of the free market and economic globalization has been seen to provide an 'overarching frame-work for Britain's political economy' (Esland *et al.* 1999: 2). The reliance on human capital notions is increasingly used as a panacea for all our economic and social problems. At the same time, increasing calls for accountability of publicly funded services have resulted in an inspection regime that has doubted the capacity of those employed in any particular government-funded service to regulate its own affairs. This suspicion has recently receded, and the new discourse around self-evaluation, a focus on the service user and the rationalization of inspection in complex services are welcome developments.

If we look at the current documentation on quality, which is dispersed amongst recent publications such as the two White Papers on Skills and 14–19 (DfES 2005b, 2005c), and the creation of the QIA, we can see that there is a change in discourse from compliance to self-regulation. There is an implicit acknowledgement that the previous inspection regimes have been excessive and that a more streamlined approach is required. This can now take as given the sector-wide picture that previous quality assurance processes established, and individual institutions can now assume responsibility for improving standards in a more autonomous way.

It may be that the creation of a workforce development programme that includes management and leadership was a necessary condition for this trust in the system to be offered. It is also the case that the cost of quality assurance is immense, and it is no surprise that one of the key components of future inspection regimes is value for money.

It is interesting that the consultation on the creation of the QIA did not draw a range of cynical responses from inspection-weary principals and senior managers. Instead, respondents identified a need for a quango that could *help* individual institutions to achieve quality.

Analysis of the current picture, then, suggests that policies are beginning to become more 'joined up', particularly about this important aspect of the sector's remit. There is an acknowledgement that the 'carrot' approach may be more effective and that success should be celebrated and, more importantly, disseminated. The challenge for the QIA, and for the sector, remains huge: to create a system in which stakeholders such as the DfES, QCA, awarding bodies, LSC, Local authorities, and, of course, learners themselves can be confident that learning and skills provision is appropriate, effective and of good quality.

7 Moving forward

'It is remarkable that – in spite of the radical and dramatic changes which have transformed education and training in general and the [Learning and Skills Sector] in particular in recent times – there has been very little discussion of the overarching values framework in which all this development has taken place.' (Lumby and Foskett 2005: 162)

The title of this book makes an impossible claim. Readers will be aware that the current pace of change in the learning and skills sector means that, even at the time of writing this book, I cannot offer an analysis of the latest policy initiative, as this will be unfolding after the book has gone to press. Having identified just a few of the major areas of policy affecting the sector, I would like to try and anticipate in this last chapter where I think the challenges lie in the coming years, and to examine what the implications are for managers in FE.

Ongoing and new initiatives

Skills Academies
What is being implemented currently? We have Skills Academies, which are following the introduction of school-based Academies, of which there are currently 17 already in existence. The Skills Academies will be public–private enterprises with employers from the business network as key participants. The aim of the Skills Academies is to help employers identify the skills they need, but also to form a 'one-stop brokerage centre', which can provide advice and guidance on the most appropriate provision in the locality. The idea of 'brokerage' is very strong in the latest Skills White Paper, moving on from the

notion of provision to advice about provision. Another form of Skills Academy will offer tuition focusing on one employment sector. All types of academy would benchmark the delivery of skills training to young people and adults.

Once again, this new policy initiative needs to be examined in relation to a previous and now fairly well established one: the Centres of Vocational Excellence (COVEs). These COVEs have been created by providers expending a great deal of energy and management resources. It will be interesting to see if the new Skills Academies will divert funding away from these or work alongside them. As Besley noted (2005c: 2), an interesting example of one Skills Academy is a Retail Academy created by Philip Green, owner of Arcadia, which will be working with 16–18-year-olds with Fashion Retail Diplomas at levels 2 and 3, through the London College of Fashion. Green is not interested in traditional A levels, but those other important aspects of learning: being 'aware, alert and alive' (ibid.).

Overarching issues

Agenda for Change, Foster and Leitch

Any of the initiatives noted above needs to be contextualized in a much wider picture. There are three issues that may require fundamental change in the sector. These will result from the LSC's analysis of its future activities, *Agenda for Change* (LSC 2005), the review of FE conducted by Sir Andrew Foster (2005), and the review of skills conducted by Lord Sandy Leitch (2006).

Agenda for Change

The LSC published its prospectus in August 2005. The Minister of State for Higher Education and Lifelong Learning, Bill Rammell, argues in the foreword that 'FE's moment has come'.

Mark Hayson, Chief Executive of the Learning and Skills Council, argued that, as the leading government agency in the FE sector, the LSC has to play an active role that must move away from micromanagement to support. He acknowledged that an effective learning and skills market must have something between 'big government and local communities'. He suggested that too much 'top down' influence results in a local system with little autonomy or sensitivity to local needs, in which managers are constrained. Too much 'bottom up' and provision is haphazard, with gaps in the curriculum, and national and regional agendas are not met. The result is the prospectus, with an agenda that has six themes.

- Creating colleges that are valued by employers as the 'partner of choice' for developing the skills they need.
- Improving the quality of provision, funding excellence and promoting the very best to serve as beacons to others.
- Simplifying radically the funding methodology and allocation process.
- Sweeping away the complexity that causes colleges to divert resources to collecting data of variable benefit.
- Developing capital investment strategy and supporting improved management systems and processes to improve business excellence.
- Working with colleges to identify ways to enable them to secure their reputation as pivotal in delivering the education and training needs of the UK. (LSC 2005: iii)

Of interest to managers, no doubt, is the promise of a simplification of funding. Those who have long memories from the early FEFC days will recognize some of the proposals, which will involve funding linked explicitly to college plans, and a core and commissioned funding model. However, the proposal to introduce a standard learner number and a provider factor will take advantage of current technology, to enable funding decisions to be made on the basis of the data arising from being able to track individual learners through the system wherever and whenever they engage in learning opportunities.

The second proposal that will affect managers is that data will be collected through a 'data partner', thereby reducing the number of multiple requests for data from a variety of sources, and linking the data back to the funding methodology.

A quality mark will be developed with employers, so that they will know what standard of services they are being offered. The National Employer Training Programme (NETP) proposed in the Skills White Paper is expected to be a powerful, demand-led mechanism for changing the way that training is offered to adults. Throughout the proposal, the discourse of self-management is strong. Words such as self-assessment, peer-referencing, self-regulation and benchmarking appear throughout. Acceleration of development of a culture of improvement through the QIA's improvement strategy is one example of how the prospectus acknowledges existing policy initiatives and builds upon them. The prospectus argues for attention to reputation as the 'golden thread' that draws the six aspects together. The prospectus is bold, self-critical, and anticipates the questions set by the Foster Review (see below). It identifies action required in sections entitled 'what we need to do' and sets out 'next steps' for each of the six themes. So how does this relate to the Foster Review?

Foster Review
Sir Andrew Foster identified early on in his review that there were positive features of the sector as well as areas for concern. The further education sector serves a vital social and economic purpose, has committed staff, good community links, adapts to national and local demand and receives positive feedback from learners. However, it has an over-heavy regulatory and accountability structure, multiple objectives, problems with funding and capital resources, an 'absence of esteem and reputation' and a fragmented qualification system.

To begin to identify how best to help the sector gain clarity and purpose, Foster set out a series of questions:

- What is the main purpose of further education colleges?
- How could the management and accountability system be clarified?
- How could learners' experiences be improved?
- How could college engagement with employers be strengthened and improved?
- How could quality improvement be driven for colleges?
- How could corporate governance be developed for colleges?
- How can the FE sector build its esteem and reputation?
- What aspects of 'workforce needs' need attention?

- How can FE colleges develop vocational pathways as outlined in the 14–19 White Paper?
- How can leadership of the sector be developed?

The answers that Foster sought aimed to help create a sector that has a core set of values uniting a diverse range of providers, a culture in which FE college staff are respected for their achievements, and one in which there will be an end to reorganization for its own sake.

His recommendations were published in *Realizing the Potential: A Review of the Future Role of Further Education Colleges* in November 2005. He set out his view using what will probably become a new metaphor for further education, that the sector is 'not a Cinderella but a middle child with huge potential that everyone has overlooked' and, furthermore, he argued that 'it does itself no favours by moaning' (Foster 2005: 58). Foster recognizes that FE has 'suffered from too many initiatives' (page 6) and despite incorporation in 1993 being celebrated by many as 'a defining moment of liberation', FE has been left 'without clear local or national incentives or constraints'. However, the report also recognizes the achievement of FE, with its 3 million learners, its breadth of activity and its particular involvement in facilitation of social inclusion. Although the report contained a series of recommendations addressing local, national and sectoral issues, there is no 'magic bullet' solution to FE (page 8).

Foster sets out a vision, a platform for change, imperatives for achievement, analysis of improvement of management and funding, analysis of improvement of inspection and information and reduction of qualifications bureaucracy, and identification of implementation to manage the change recommended. His review has been well received by the sector and, it would appear, by government. What are the primary issues arising from his report?

Perhaps the most fundamental change that Foster is recommending is that FE needs to become known for expertise in one major area, that of fostering skills in the workplace. It should therefore help meet the needs of the economy but also develop its own workforce. He argues that FE has tried to be all

things to all people, which has led to 'mission drift' and confusion amongst stakeholders who could benefit from the services that FE should provide.

Once a clear mission has been identified, the other changes,
reducing bureaucracy, improving the gathering of data and
ensuring that the sector is appropriately managed and funded,
fall into place. Thus, the newly proposed system of inspection,
through the merger of ALI and Ofsted, and less centralization
but more self-regulation, should enable the sector to be more
effective and efficient in its self-management. Foster also
identified the need to create a more systematic and coherent
information-gathering process, and recommended that there
should be a single data agency covering both FE and HE that
would rationalize and simplify data collection.

There are some strong messages for underperforming colleges, which unfortunately became the focus of much of the
reporting in the press immediately following the publication of
the Foster Review, despite acknowledging that the majority of
teaching and provision has been judged to be of good or even
high quality.

Leitch

The Government announced in 2004 that Sandy Leitch had
been asked to lead an independent review to examine the
future skills needs of the UK economy. This review, the Leitch
Review of Skills, is due to report back to Government in spring
2006, on the skills profile the UK should aim to achieve by
2020 to support productivity and economic growth as well as
social objectives over the long term. The Review has worked
with a wide range of stakeholders to build an evidence base
upon which the government can set its ambitions for 2020 and
will consider the implications for skills policy.

The document *Skills in the Global Economy* describes the
social and economic problems apparently 'caused' by adults in
the UK without basic skills; the need for a highly skilled
workforce to confront the challenges posed by global markets;
and the UK's relatively poor international position in intermediate level skills.

The terms of reference published alongside the 2004 Pre-Budget Report are:

- to examine the UK's optimum skills mix in order to maximize economic growth and productivity by 2020
- in particular, to consider the different trajectories of skills levels the UK might pursue.

The Review is asked to address the following key questions:

- What is the current trajectory for the development of skills in the UK and therefore the likely profile of skills in 2020?
- What will be the optimal skills mix in 2020 (for example, in relation to economic and social objectives)? The feasibility and cost of implementing policy; and international comparisons.
- What trajectories can the UK pursue in order to achieve this skills profile by 2020?
- What are the implications for policy?

At the time of writing, the review has not yet been completed but the Leich interim report was published in December 2005 (see www.hm-treasury.gov.uk/leitch). Readers should consult the Treasury website for recent releases of information.

Challenges, opportunities and change

What are the challenges, then, facing the sector? The Association of Colleges (AoC) has identified four:

- further reform of 14–19 learning
- expansion of adult learning to meet the emerging demographic shift
- more resources and a more intelligent attitude to regulation and risk
- increased spending on post-16 education, from 2 per cent to 2.5 per cent of GDP.

More widely, the interdependency between a college and its local economy needs to be recognized, taking into account changes in demography, migrant skills and the changing needs of employers as they, too, work in an interdependent context of local, regional, national and global factors.

If we examine these four challenges, we can see that they, too, are interdependent. For example, the 14–19 reform includes the continuing debates around the qualifications framework, how to reconcile vocational versus academic goals, working with employers, disparities between conditions of service between FE and school staff and strategies to ensure staff in the FE sector are qualified to teach young people. If we focus on adult learners, similar issues arise, but this time, the issues are to do with the Framework for Achievement, the Skills White Paper, and funding. Regulation and risk covers the whole of the learning and skills sector, and the emerging prospectus for change published by LSC in August 2005 acknowledges how much the sector has been subject to the vagaries of funding since incorporation in 1993. Finally, any public service calls for additional spending: the learning and skills sector is not alone in this. Yet the targets set are bold and demanding, and simply cannot be met without the necessary funding.

An example of the interdependency of issues can be seen in the funding crisis for adult learners that took place in the summer of 2005. National Institute of Adult and Continuing Education (NIACE) identified that every extra place for a 16–18-year-old learner results in ten fewer places for adult learners. The concentration on funding a full level 2 or basic skills qualification meant that the funding pot could not pay for everyone else. The cash crisis led some FE colleges to pulp their adult learning prospectuses when they were informed that they would not be receiving the level of funding they were expecting for this important group of people. The 10.3 per cent increase in funding for 16–18-year-olds led to a cut of 3 per cent for adult learners. As most colleges needed 5 per cent growth this year just to maintain their current provision, the outcome is, in effect, an 8 per cent cut, which affected the 3.5 million adults registered for programmes of learning in summer 2005. The crisis was such that a debate in the House of Commons in June 2005 was 'exceptionally well-attended' (*Education and Training Monitor* 2005).

The former Secretary of State for Education, Ruth Kelly,

made it clear that her priority is to fund level 2 qualifications as 'the platform for career and life' (Kelly, LSDA Annual Conference, June 2005), with a clear expectation that employers must contribute more to the cost for level 3 qualifications. She further argued that 'we have to find a new balance of responsibilities between the duty of government and the responsibilities of learners and employers'. It is interesting how close this comment is to the original statements made in the Green Paper *The Learning Age* in 1998.

Staff in the sector

The key to the implementation of any policy, government review and resultant recommendations is the staff who have to undertake the lion's share of introducing change. The biggest challenge, then, following the Foster and Leitch reviews, and the Agenda for Change, is to engage the staff in FE to implement local recommendations for change. At the time of writing, FE staff conditions of service are worse than those in schools, their teaching qualifications do not yet give them qualified teacher status, and they are overwhelmingly casualized by comparison with the compulsory sector.

How can staff be motivated and engaged? Managers and leaders hold a key responsibility to equip their staff to meet the challenges set out above. As Barry Quirk (LSDA Conference, June 2005) noted, 'stewarding the life chances of young people into an unknowable future is awesome'. If staff are to do this effectively, they need effective management and leadership.

Managers, then, have an onerous responsibility. They need to work on four levels:

- national (economic management)
- organizational (strategic management)
- service (operational management)
- practitioner (operational management).

If there is no leadership, their management is like strategy without operation. In other words, as Barry Quirk argued, it is a fantasy (LSDA Conference, June 2005).

At national level, we can see that the challenge is partially down to the short period of tenure that lifelong learning ministers have held. For example, we have had seven ministers since 1997, in a situation in which 'policymakers suffer from a terminal policy amnesia' (Ken Spours, plenary presentation, LSE LSRN Annual Conference, July 2005). This led Frank Coffield to suggest that the incoming government following the 2005 election should appoint a lifelong minister of learning, 'or at least a minister of learning who stays in the post for a full four years. Not exactly a lifetime ... but it would be a start' (Coffield 2005).

Managers in FE will be working primarily at the organizational, service and practitioner level. Jameson (2006) and Jameson and McNay (forthcoming 2007) discuss how best to address the management and leadership practices required successfully to undertake the responsibilities outlined above.

However, let's explore some positive aspects of the sector. The third LSC National Learner Satisfaction Survey, which examined provision in 2003/4, asked over 31,000 learners core questions about their overall satisfaction with the quality of teaching and management of learning. Ninety-one per cent were satisfied with the quality of teaching, of whom 24 per cent were extremely satisfied. Learners appreciated that their tutors knew the subject and related to learners as people. Sixty-one per cent were satisfied with the experience of learning and 87 per cent indicated that they were likely overall to return to further learning within the next three years. The sector enjoys substantial government funding with £10 billion allocated for 2005–2008, and in 2005 an additional £350 million for capital investment for the period 2008–2010 has been allocated to support the long-term transformation of the FE sector. The challenges may be great, but the government interest in the sector is clearly demonstrated in the number of policies it creates and in the use of levers such as funding to steer a course for meeting the goals of prosperity, mobility and justice articulated by the Secretary of State for Education.

How have we done so far?

Let us return now to the original overarching policy framework, Success for All. In 2004, the DfES commissioned a feasibility study to measure the extent of the impact of Success for All initiatives from cross-cutting themes in the Public Service Agreement (PSA) targets, and the relative impact of Success for All initiatives, other policy effects and external factors in the theme-level targets. The study found that absolute attribution of Success for All impact was not possible, but relative attribution was. In other words, links could be found between the four themes of Success for All and PSA targets, but it was not possible to say that it was because of the initiative that the targets had been met. What is interesting about this study is that it recognized how difficult it is to measure any particular policy and its impact, as there are so many other policies that affect its outcomes.

The study mapped indicators of impact and created an evaluation framework for the themes. It developed a grid, which showed how there were combined effects that were integrative or contradictory on a number of aspects of Success for All. For example, there was synergy between the Strategic Area Reviews (StARs), COVEs and sixth-form provision. There was close integration between reforming teaching pedagogy, and management and training through the reform of initial teacher training, and the creation of the Centre for Excellence in Leadership. There were links between three-year funding and development planning with initiatives requiring investment over time, such as pedagogy and training initiatives that required large-scale diffusion processes to achieve full impact.

There were, though, contradictions. There were time-related contradictions between the initiatives requiring long-term investment and medium-term structural change. (For example, there were tensions between StARs and time-reliant initiatives.) There were contradictions because of geographical factors, for example between provider-level and area-level priorities. There were outcome-related contradictions, for example between widening participation and performance-related funding, in which activities responding to Entry to Employment (E2E) might not have favourable impact on success rates, which were key to funding.

The analysis identified that some targets were seen as more urgent, high-profile or important than others, but others were difficult to measure or achieve. The model created in the analysis identified three tiers: core targets, contributor targets or milestones and programme effects. For example, in Tier One, targets related to success rates and inspection results, and the criteria used to help identify whether they met the PSA cross-cutting targets included the fundamental aims of Success for All and how robust and verifiable they were.

The model helps to clarify the likely phasing of impacts within a theme, but also patterns of impact. Thus in 2003 a plateau effect was observed, as a number of initiatives were launched including the setting up of CEL, the reform of Initial Teacher Training (ITT), the National Coaching Programme and Professional Subject Networks. There was a further period of impetus when the reform of HE took hold, with its new Professional Standards, as well as new skills and qualifications for e-business and e-learning coinciding with this period.

There is a more general accumulation effect, and the report suggests that it is important to collect data to take account of the 'bedding-down' process, as interventions become established. The model can help become a forecasting and validation tool. Why is this report, then, so important? It provides, perhaps for the first time, an acknowledgement that initiatives and policies are difficult to 'pin down' in terms of their impact, and that a means of identifying how they interact and more importantly contradict each other is necessary, to take appropriate action to prevent policy drift. They also help identify where policy is being enacted differently, for example where there is a strong local dimension, as some common initiatives do not always assume the same level of importance within local LSCs at any one point in time. The analysis can help highlight 'entanglement', where individual initiatives combine to re-enforce a process, or multiple sources of activity are implicated within any one particular impact. For example, a curriculum mapping process is clearly linked to improved option choice for 16–18-year-olds in one LSC, but this is also supported by area-wide action planning, 14–19 strategies and increased flexibility. It would be impossible to specify the cause and effect of each of these initiatives on the resultant activity.

What is useful, though, is the ability to study combinations of initiatives and identify which clusters of initiatives, under what conditions, work best together. This seems to me to be of huge potential. Instead of working across initiatives in a reactive way, it would be possible to draw together strategies to ensure that policies could work together, and also identify where there are going to be tensions and contradictions. This is something that most managers spot intuitively, but a systematic analysis provides more information and enables an informed approach to managing what will be challenging issues in the implementation of the initiatives.

It is here that the Foster Report (2005) has most potential to help create a more coherent, systemic approach to providing learning opportunities for millions of people. Foster rightly recognized that FE suffered from too many initiatives, has been unhelpfully seen as a sector and would benefit from being addressed as a system that can respond to learner, societal and economic needs (2005: 10). He understood that reforms such as those introduced by the Learning and Skills Act (2000) merely 'layered a new arrangement on top of old systems' (page 17). Even the freedom that FE colleges gained in deciding what to deliver after incorporation in 1993 resulted in 'ever more interventionist roles to re-balance the market in post-compulsory education between providers and learners', as well as isolating the institutions because they became competitive rather than collaborative. Furthermore, Foster identified the 'squeeze' that FE colleges experienced in the changing landscape of school, FE and HE sectors. Thus, thinking about FE in relation to the whole education system needs policy steers from the DfES that will help learners to have provision that is coherent. The important 'architectural' role of government, therefore, is vital to help the system move away from its bounded territory with its internecine struggles. As Ruth Kelly noted in her key speech at the AoC conference in November 2005, there are five key strands to the approach that the DfES must take, of mission and purpose, specialization, responsiveness, ensuring quality and autonomy and accountability. At the time of writing, the Foster Report has yet to be endorsed and implemented, but the sector has received an endorsement for its strengths that should help it move towards more effective provision.

Back to the future

It is interesting to see how policy analysts make predictions about the FE sector and, because they invariably cannot make accurate forecasts, I do not intend to replicate their errors. But it is worth examining what was written about the future of FE six years ago.

Lifelong learning was a key theme for many commentators on education policy for the FE sector. The role of government in encouraging participation was seen as one that would steer the more liberal aims of helping people learn what they wanted towards learning that would 'count', as Jarvis argued:

> 'Governments clearly seek to influence the market through devising strategies which will be funding-based but, since there are now no monopoly providers in a global situation, they can do so only through what they will fund and the awards that they will recognize. There is, however, a danger in this situation since it is possible that only learning that is recognized by some form of award becomes defined as the "real" learning, while all the other human learning that helps make people what they are will be neglected and regarded as unreal, even unnecessary, and lifelong learning will become equated with worklife learning.' (Jarvis 2005: 63)

Hodgson and Spours suggested that the approach to lifelong learning in England represented a 'weak framework approach' in which emphasis was placed on the individual without dealing with the fundamental barriers to participation and achievement. By contrast, in Wales and Scotland, there was a 'strong framework approach', which took account of individuals who could fulfil their individual aspirations, but which also acknowledged that there needed to be phased progress for the participation of a wider range of people over a longer timescale. They argued that:

> 'The role of government is to articulate a vision for lifelong learning and to put into place an infrastructure of strong frameworks to encourage participation, progression and achievement ... One of the functions of compulsory education should not only be to provide the basic skills to cope

changes in the control system, the workforce profile and the curriculum offering which defines each education and training organization have served only to further embed the values and social class differentials which pre-existed. Government has conducted elaborate rites, in which scapegoats such as LEAs and teachers have been identified, but the changes ultimately confirm the status quo.' (Lumby and Foskett 2005: 43)

This book has begun to identify how different policies that have profound implications for FE swirl around each other as people plot their way through mist and fog, sometimes clearing enough for them to see their way clearly, and often finding their view obscured. A sensible walker takes a map, compass, food, water and protective clothing. The sensible manager in FE needs, then, to know what policies exist and what their aims are, to identify a sensible route, which may have to change when obstacles are encountered, and to be prepared for changes in conditions at very short notice. I hope that this approach to analysing policy, by examining the consequences, predicting unintended consequences, and, most importantly, being aware of the agency each of us possesses, will enable readers to continue their journeys into the future policy spaces that await them.

Postscript

The White Paper *Further Education: Raising Skills, Improving Life Chances* was published in March 2006. It takes on board many of the recommendations made by Sir Andrew Foster and once again provides important signals to the FE sector on government policy. Even in the foreword and executive summary there are clear indications in the language used that the role of FE is to be a provider of skills to the nation. For example, in his foreword the Prime Minister argues that FE should be a 'powerhouse of a high skills economy'. Furthermore, the paper claims that the government will 'put the economic mission of the sector at the heart of its role' (page 6). Throughout the document there are strong words, emphasis on decisive action and a mission to compete with world standards. There are six key areas set out in a programme of change for FE:

- Strengthening the focus of the system on a core economic mission.
- Greater focus of that mission on meeting the needs and demands of learners and employers.
- Ensuring quality of learning and teaching is uniformly excellent across the sector.
- Using a more robust framework of intervention to support poor quality.
- Reconfiguration of funding and organization of the sector.
- New relationship with colleges and other providers.

By the time this book is published, the period of consultation will be over and the DfES will have begun its programme of implementation. As you have read throughout this book, policy in FE is intricately bound up with other policy creation and implementation. There will be much fallout from the latest government White Paper and you, the reader, will have your part to play in this continually evolving policy framework. I hope that your actions will now be informed by a greater understanding of what policy is and that you will continue to develop your professional practice in ways that value and respect your learners and your colleagues.

Glossary and useful acronyms

ABSSU	Adult Basic Skills Strategy Unit
ACVE	Advanced Certificate in Vocational Education
ALI	Adult Learning Inspectorate
ALLN	Adult Literacy, Language and Numeracy
ALM	Adults Learning Mathematics
AoC	Association of Colleges
BSA	Basic Skills Agency
BTF	Bureaucracy Task Force
CBI	Confederation of British Industry
CEL	Centre for Excellence in Leadership
COVE	Centre of Vocational Excellence
CPD	Continuing Professional Development
CPVE	Certificate in Pre-vocational Education
CQFW	Credit and Qualification Framework for Wales
CSE	Certificate in Secondary Education
DES	Department of Education and Science
DfEE	Department for Education and Employment
DfES	Department for Education and Skills
DPA	Deliberative policy analysis
DTI	Department of Trade and Industry
DWP	Department for Work and Pensions
ED	Employment Department
EMA	Education Maintenance Allowance
ERA	Education Reform Act
ESOL	English for Speakers of Other Languages
E2E	Entry to Employment
ET	Employment Training
EU	European Union
FE	Further Education
FEDA	Further Education Development Agency
FEFC	Further Education Funding Council
FENTO	Further Education National Training Organization

FEU	Further Education Unit
FfA	Framework for Achievement
FRESA	Framework for Regional Employment and Skills Action
GCE	General Certificate of Education
GCSE	General Certificate of Secondary Education
GNVQ	General National Vocational Qualification
HE	Higher Education
HEFCE	Higher Education Funding Council for England
HMI	Her Majesty's Inspectorate
HND	Higher National Diploma
IALS	International Adult Literacy Survey
ICT	Information and Communications Technology
IfL	Institute for Learning
ITT	Initial Teacher Training
LEA	Local Education Authority
LLU	Language and Literacy Unit (South Bank University)
LLUK	Lifelong Learning Sector Skills Council
LSC	Learning and Skills Council
LSDA	Learning and Skills Development Agency
MA	Modern Apprenticeships
MSC	Manpower Services Commission
NAFE	Non-advanced Further Education
NAGCELL	National Advisory Group for Continuing Education and Lifelong Learning
NAO	National Audit Office
NATFHE	National Association of Teachers in Further and Higher Education
NCDS	National Child Development Survey
NCVQ	National Council for Vocational Qualifications
NEET	Not in Education, Employment or Training
NETP	National Employer Training Pilot
NETTs	National Education and Training Targets
NIACE	National Institute for Adult and Continuing Education
NICATS	Northern Ireland Credit Accumulation and Transfer Scheme
NOCN	National Open College Network
NPQH	National Professional Qualification for Headship
NRDC	National Research and Development Centre for Adult Literacy, Numeracy and ESOL
NTO	National Training Organization
NVQ	National Vocational Qualification

OECD	Organization for Economic Cooperation and Development
Ofsted	Office for Standards in Education
PAULO	Adult Education National Training Organization
PCET	Post-compulsory Education and Training
PGCE	Postgraduate Certificate in Education
PISA	Programme for International Student Assessment
QCA	Qualifications and Curriculum Authority
QIA	Quality Improvement Agency
QTS	Qualified Teacher Status
QTLS	Qualified Teacher Learning and Skills
RaPAL	Research and Practice in Adult Literacy
RSA	Royal Society of Arts
SBC	Small Business Council
SCQF	Scottish Credit and Qualification Framework
SENET	Skills and Education Network
SK4L	Skills for Life
SSC	Sector Skills Council
StAR	Strategic Area Review
TA	Training Agency
TEC	Training and Enterprise Council
TOPS	Training Opportunities Scheme
TUC	Trades Union Congress
TVEI	Technical and Vocational Education Initiative
UfI	University for Industry
YOPS	Youth Opportunities Scheme
YT	Youth Training
YTS	Youth Training Scheme

Useful websites

Adult Learning Inspectorate
www.ali.org.uk

Basic Skills Agency
www.basic-skills.co.uk

BBC Skillswise
www.bbc.co.uk/skillswise

Campaign for Learning
www.campaign-for-learning.org.uk

Connexions
www.connexions.gov.uk

Department for Education and Skills (DfES)
www.dfes.gov.uk

Improvement and Development Agency (IDeA)
www.idea.gov.uk

Institute for Learning (IfL)
www.ifl.org.uk

Learning and Skills Council
www.lsc.gov.uk

Lifelong Learning UK
www.lifelonglearning.org.uk

National Institute of Adult and Continuing Education
www.niace.org.uk

National Open College Network
www.nocn.org.uk

National Research and Development Centre for Adult Literacy,
Numeracy and ESOL (NRDC)
www.nrdc.org.uk

Office for Standards in Education (Ofsted)
www.ofsted.gov.uk

Organization for Economic Cooperation and Development (OECD)
www.oecd.org

Qualifications and Curriculum Authority (QCA)
www.qca.org.uk

United Nations Educational, Scientific and Cultural Organization
(UNESCO)
www.unesco.org/education

University for Industry (UfI)
www.ufi.org.uk

Bibliography

Adult Learning Inspectorate (ALI)/Office for Standards in Education (Ofsted) (2001) *Common Inspection Framework*, London: ALI/Ofsted.

Adult Learning Inspectorate (ALI)/Office for Standards in Education (Ofsted) (2005) *Common Inspection Framework*, London: ALI/Ofsted. See www.ofsted.gov.uk/www.ali.gov.uk (accessed February 2006).

Ainley, P. (2003) 'Towards a seamless web or a new tertiary tripartism? The emerging shape of post-14 education and training in England', *British Journal of Educational Studies*, 51 (4): 390–407.

Allison, G. T. (1971) *The Essence of Decision: Explaining the Cuban Missile Crisis*, Boston, MA: Little Brown.

Almond, G. A., Powerll, G. B. and Mundt, R. J. (1993) *Comparative Politics: A Theoretical Framework*, New York: HarperCollins.

Bailey, B. and Ainley, P. (2000) in D. Gray and C. Griffin (eds) *Postcompulsory Education and the New Millennium*, Higher Education Policy series 54, London: Jessica Kingsley Publications.

Barrett, S. and Fudge, C. (eds) (1981) *Policy and Action: Essays on the Implementation of Public Policy*, London: Methuen.

Basic Skills Agency (2004) 'Is it true?', *Basic Skills*, Summer 2004, London: BSA.

Benn, C. and Fairley, J. (eds) (1986) *Challenging the MSC on Jobs, Education and Training: Enquiry into a National Disaster*, London: Pluto Press.

Besley, S. (2003) *Success for All: The First Year*, Policy Briefing, London: Edexcel.

Besley, S. (2005a) *Policy Watch*, 23 March 2005, London: Edexcel.

Besley, S. (2005b) *Policy Watch*, 29 March 2005, London: Edexcel.

Besley, S. (2005c) *Policy Watch 39*, 19 May 2005, London: Edexcel.

Besley, S. (2005d) *Policy Watch*, June 2005, London: Edexcel.

Besley, S. (2005e) *Policy Watch*, July 2005, London: Edexcel.

Betts, D. (2000) 'A functional analysis of the part-time lecturing staff in FE colleges in England and Wales; their roles and characteristics', London: FENTO.

Bloomer, M. (1997) *Curriculum Making in Post-16 Education*, London: Routledge.

Bourdieu, P. (1977) *Outline of a Theory of Practice*, Cambridge: Cambridge University Press.

Bourdieu, P. (1993) *Sociology in Question*, London: Sage.

Bourdieu, P. and Passeron, J. (1977) *Reproduction in Education, Society and Culture* (trans. R. Nice), London: Sage.

Brookfield, S. D. (1995) *Becoming a Critically Reflective Teacher*, San Francisco: Jossey Bass.

Brown, G. (2005) *Investing in our Future*, DfES, London: The Stationery Office.

Burgess, T. (1964) *A Guide to English Schools*, Harmondsworth: Penguin.

Bynner, J. and Parsons, S. (1997) *It Doesn't get any Better: The Impact of Poor Basic Skills on the Lives of 37-year-olds*, London: Basic Skills Agency.

Cantor, L., Roberts, I. F. and Pratley, B. (1995) *A Guide to Further Education in England and Wales*, London: Cassells.

Chanda, N. (2005) 'Issues in adult numeracy', *Reflect*, no. 2, February 2005, pp4–7.

Chitty, C. (2000) 'Vocational education and training into the new millennium' in D. Gray and C. Griffin (eds) *Post-compulsory Education and the New Millennium*, London: Jessica Kingsley.

Coben, D. (2001) 'Fact, fiction and moral panic: the changing adult numeracy curriculum in England', *Adult and Lifelong Education in Mathematics*, Papers from Working Group for Action 69th International Congress on Mathematical Education (ICME) Melbourne.

Coben, D. (2006, forthcoming) 'The politics of numeracy: a sociocultural approach to adult numeracy: issues for policy and practice' in L. Tett, M. Hamilton and Y. Hillier, *Adult Literacy, Numeracy and Language: Policy, Practice and Research*, Maidenhead: McGraw Hill.

Cockett, M. and Callaghan, J. (1996) 'Caught in the middle – transition at 16+' in R. Halsall and M. Cockett (eds) *Education and Training 14–19: Chaos or Coherence?*, London: David Fulton.

Coffield, F. (2005) 'Lifelong learning', letter in the *Guardian*, Tuesday 19 April (www.educationguardian.co.uk/schools special reports/lifelong learning, accessed 8 September 2005).

Cohen, M., March, J. and Olsen, J. (1972) 'A garbage can model of organisational choice', *Administrative Science Quarterly*, 17: 1–25.

Crowther Report (1959) *15 to 18 Report of the Central Advisory Council for Education (England)*, vol. 1, report; vol. 2, statistics, London: HMSO.

Dass, P. and Parker, B. (1999) 'Strategies for managing human resource diversity: from resistance to learning', *Academy of Management Executive* 13 (2): 68–80.

Department for Education and Employment (DfEE) (1997) *Qualifying for Success*, London: HMSO.

Department for Education and Employment (DfEE) (1998) *The Learning Age: Renaissance for a New Britain*, Green Paper Cmnd 3790, London: Stationery Office.

Department for Education and Employment (DfEE) (1999a) *Learning to Succeed: A New Framework for Post-16 Learning*, London: Stationery Office.

Department for Education and Employment (DfEE) (1999b) *National Skills Task Force: Towards a National Skills Agenda*, London: Stationery Office.

Department for Education and Employment (DfEE) (2000a) *Tackling the Adult Skills Gap*, London: Stationery Office.

Department for Education and Employment (DfEE) (2000b) *Colleges for Excellence and Innovation*, London: Stationery Office.

Department for Education and Skills (DfES) (2001) *Skills for Life: The National Strategy for Improving Adult Literacy and Numeracy Skills*, London: DfES.

Department for Education and Skills (DfES) (2002) *Success for All: Reforming Further Education and Training*, London: Stationery Office.

Department for Education and Skills (DfES) (2003) *Realising our Potential – Individuals, Employers, Nation* (www.dfes.gov.uk/skillstrategy/docs/fulldoc.pdf), July 2003.

Department for Education and Skills (DfES) (2004) *Standards Unit: National Quality Improvement Body for the Learning and Skills Sector Progress Report, 16 November 2004*, London: DfES.

Department for Education and Skills (DfES) (2005a) *Standards Unit Newsletter*, Issue 9, Summer 2005, London: DfES.

Department for Education and Skills (DfEs) (2005b) *Skills: Getting on in Business, Getting on at Work*, London: DfES.

Department for Education and Skills (DfES) (2005c) *14–19 Education and Skills*, London: DfES.

Department for Education and Skills (DfES) (2006) *Further Education: Revising Skills, Improving Life Chances*, London: HMSO.

Department of Education and Science/Department of Employment (1991) *Education and Training for the 21st Century*, London: HMSO.

Department of Employment (1981) *A New Training Initiative: Programme for Action*, Cmnd 8455, London: HMSO.

Department of Employment (1986) *Working Together: Education and Training*, London: HMSO.

Department of Employment (1989) *Employment for the 1990s*, London: HMSO.

Dror, Y. (1967) 'Policy analysis: a new professional role in government service', *Public Administration Review*, 27 (3): 197–203.

Easton, D. (1965) *A Framework for Political Analysis*, Englewood Cliffs NJ: Prentice-Hall.

ECOTEC Research and Consulting Ltd (2005) *Evaluation of Success for All: Attributing Impact to Specific Themes/Initiatives*, Birmingham: ECOTEC.

Education and Training Monitor (2005) 'Huge turnout for "funding crisis" debate', Croydon: Cadmus Newsletters.

Esland, G., Flude, M. and Sieminski, S. (eds) (1999) Introduction, *Education, Training and the Future of Work 11: Developments in Vocational Education and Training*, London: Routledge/Open University Press.

Etzioni, A. (1968) *The Active Society: A Theory of Societal and Political Processes*, New York: Free Press.

European Union (2000a) *Memorandum on Lifelong Learning*, Brussels: EU.

European Union (2000b) *Lisbon Agenda*, Brussels: EU.

Fawbert, F. (ed.) (2003) *Teaching in Post-compulsory Education: Learning, Skills and Standards*, London: Continuum.

Field, J. (1996) 'Learning for work: vocational education and training' in R. Fieldhouse (ed.) *A History of Modern British Adult Education*, Leicester: NIACE, 353.

Field, J. (2000) *Lifelong Learning and the New Education Order*, Stoke-on-Trent: Trentham.

Fieldhouse, R. (ed.) (1996) *A History of Modern British Adult Education*, Leicester: NIACE.

Finegold, D. (1993) 'The emerging post-16 system: analysis and criteria' in W. Richardson, J. Woolhouse and D. Finegold (eds) (1993) *The Reform of Post-16 Education and Training in England and Wales*, Harlow: Longman.

Finegold, D. and Soskice, D. (1988) 'The failure of training in Britain' in G. Esland (ed.) *Education, Training and Employment*, Milton Keynes: Open University Press.

Fischer, F. and Forrester, F. (1993) *The Argumentative Turn in Policy Analysis and Planning*, Durham, NC: Duke University Press.

Fletcher, M. (2003) 'Skills strategy – new priorities', *LSDA Briefing*, September 2003, London: LSDA.

Foster, A. (2005) *14–19 Curriculum and Qualifications Reform: Final Report of the Working Group on 14–19 Reform*, London: Stationery Office.

Foucault, M. (1970) *The Order of Things – An Archeology of the Human Sciences*, New York: Vintage Books.

Foucault, M. (1980) *Power/Knowledge: Selected Interviews and Other Writings 1972–77*, C. Gordon (ed.), Brighton: Harvester.

Further Education National Training Organization (FENTO) (1999) *Standards for Teaching and Supporting Learning in England and Wales*, London: FENTO.

Further Education Unit (FEU) (1983) *A Basis for Choice*, Blagdon: FEU.

Further Education Unit (FEU) (1995) *A Framework for Credit*, London: FEU.

Goldstein, H. (2006) 'Education for all: the globalisation of learning targets' in L. Tett, M. Hamilton and Y. Hillier (eds) (2006) *Adult Literacy, Numeracy and Language: Policy, Practice and Research*, Maidenhead: McGraw Hill.

Gramsci, A. (1994) *Letters from Prison* (ed. by F. Rosengarten; trans. R. Rosenthal), New York: Columbia Press.

Green, A. (1986) 'The MSC and the three-tier structure of further education' in C. Benn and J. Fairley (eds) (1986) *Challenging the MSC on Jobs, Education and Training: Enquiry into a National Disaster*, London: Pluto Press.

Habermas, J. (1981) *The Theory of Communicative Action: Reason and the Rationalisation of Society* (trans. T. McCarthy), Boston: Beacon Press.

Hajer, M. and Wagenaar, H. (eds) (2003) *Deliberative Policy Analysis: Understanding Government in the Network Society*, Cambridge: CUP.

Hamilton, M. (1996) 'Adult literacy and basic education' in R. Fieldhouse (ed.) *A Modern History of Adult Education*, Leicester: NIACE.

Hamilton, M. and Hillier, Y. (2006) *The Changing Faces of Adult Literacy, Language and Numeracy: A Critical History*, Stoke on Trent: Trentham.

Handy, C. (1994) *The Empty Raincoat*, London: Hutchinson.

Heclo, II. (1972) Review article: 'Policy analysis', *British Journal of Political Science*, 2: 83–108.

Herrington, M. and Kendall, A. (eds) (2005) *Insights from Research and Practice: A Handbook for Adult Literacy, Numeracy and ESOL Practitioners*, Leicester: NIACE.

Hillier, Y. (2002) *Reflective Teaching in Further and Adult Education*, London: Continuum.

Hillier, Y. (2005) *Reflective Teaching in Further and Adult Education*, 2nd edn, London: Continuum.

Hillier, Y. and Jameson, J. (2003) *Empowering Researchers in Further Education*, Stoke on Trent: Trentham.

Hillier, Y. and Jameson, J. (2004) *A Rich Contract? Or the Ragged-trousered Philanthropy of Part-time Staff: The Deployment and Development of Part-time Staff in the Learning and Skills Sector*, London: LSDA.

Hodgson, A. (2000) *Policies, Politics and the Future of Lifelong Learning*, London: Kogan Page.

Hodgson, A. and Spours, K. (eds) (1997) *Dearing and Beyond: 14–19 Qualifications and Frameworks*, London: Kogan Page.

Hodgson, A. and Spours, K. (2000) 'Building a lifelong learning system for the future' in A. Hodgson (ed.) *Policies, Politics and the Future of Lifelong Learning*, London: Kogan Page.

Hodgson, A. and Spours, K. (2002) 'Key skills for all? The key skills qualification and Curriculum 2000', *Journal of Education Policy*, 17 (1): 29–47.

Hodkinson, P., Sparkes, A. C. and Hodkinson, H. (1996) *Triumphs and Tears: Young People, Markets and the Transion from School to Work*, London: David Fulton.

Hogwood, B. W. and Gunn, L. A. (1984) *Policy Analysis for the Real World*, London: Oxford University Press.

Hoppe, R. (1993) 'Political judgement and the policy cycle: the case of ethnicity policy arguments in the Netherlands', in F. Fischer and F. Forester, (eds) *The Argumentative Turn in Policy Analysis and Planning*, London: UCL Press.

Hyland, T. and Merrill, B. (2003) *The Changing Face of Further Education: Lifelong Learning, Inclusion and Community Values in Further Education*, London: Routledge Falmer.

Jameson, J. (2006) *Leadership in Post Compulsory Education: Inspiring Leaders of the Future*, London: David Fulton.

Jarvis, P. (2000) 'Lifelong learning – an agenda for a late-modern future' in C. Griffin and D. Gray (eds) *Post-compulsory Education and the New Millennium*, London: Jessica Kingsley.

Kelly, R. (2005) *The Next Term: Priorities and Challenges for Learning and Skills*, LSDA Summer Conference 21 June 2005 verbatim transcript: Ubiqus Reporting.

Kelly, T. (1970) *A History of Adult Education in Great Britain*, Liverpool: Liverpool University Press.

Kennedy, H. (1997) *Learning Works: Widening Participation in Further Education*, Coventry: Further Education Funding Council.

Lasswell, H. D. (1956) *The Decision Process: Seven Categories of Functional Analysis*, Maryland: University of Maryland.

Lasswell, H. D. (1970) 'The emerging conception of the policy sciences', *Policy Sciences*, 1: 3–14.

Lavender, P., Derrick, J. and Brooks, B. (2004) *Testing Testing 123: Assessment in Adult Literacy, Language and Numeracy*, Leicester: NIACE.

Learning and Skills Council (2005) *Learning and Skills – the agenda for change: The Prospectus*, Coventry: LSC.

Leitch, S. (2005) *Skills in the UK: The Long-term Challenge*, Interim Report (www.dfes.gov.uk accessed February 2006).

Lindblom, C. E. (1959) 'The science of muddling through', *Public Administration Review*, 19: 78–88.

Lindblom, C. E. and Woodhouse, E. J. (1993) *The Policy-making Process*, 3rd edn, Englewood Cliffs NJ: Prentice-Hall.

Lo Bianco, J. and Freebody, P. (1997) *Australian Literacies: Informing National Policy on Literacy Education*, Melbourne: National Languages and Literacy Institute of Australia.

Lumby, J. and Foskett, N. B. (2005) *14–19 Education: Policy, Leadership and Learning*, London: Sage.

Lucas, N. (2000) 'Hopes, contradictions and challenges: lifelong learning and the further education sector' in Hodgson, A. (ed.) *Policies, Politics and the Future of Lifelong Learning*, London: Kogan Page.

Mace, J. (2002) 'Can't someone in the real world write a proper test for literacy?', the *Guardian*, Tuesday 28 May.

Marcuse, H. (1972) *One Dimensional Man*, London: Abacus.

Moser, C. (1999) *A Fresh Start: Improving Literacy and Numeracy*, London: DfEE.

National Advisory Group for Continuing Education and Lifelong Learning (NAGCELL) (1997) *Learning for the 21st Century: First Report of the National Advisory Group for Continuing Education and Lifelong Learning*, London: NAGCELL.

National Advisory Group for Continuing Education and Lifelong Learning (NAGCELL) (1999) *Creating Learning Cultures: Next Steps in Achieving the Learning Age*, London: Stationery Office.

National Audit Office (2004) *Skills for Life: Improving Adult Literacy and Numeracy*, Report by the Comptroller and Auditor General, HC 20, London: DfES.

National Institute for Adult and Continuing Education (NIACE) (2003) 'Has the government got it right?', *Adults Learning*, July 2003: 9–14.

Office for Standards in Education (Ofsted) (2003a) *Annual Report of Her Majesty's Chief Inspector of Schools Standards and Quality in Education 2001/02*, London: DfES.

Office for Standards in Education (Ofsted) (2003b) *The Initial Training of Further Education Teachers: A Survey*, London: The Stationery Office.

Office for Standards in Education (Ofsted) (2003c) *Literacy, Numeracy and English for Speakers of Other Languages: A Survey of Current Practice in Post-16 and Adult Provision*, London: Ofsted.

Organization for Economic Cooperation and Development (OECD) (1997) *Literacy Skills for the Knowledge Society*, Paris: OECD.

Organization for Economic Cooperation and Development (OECD) (2000) *Literacy in the Information Age: Final Report of the International Literacy Survey*, Paris: OECD.

Ozga, J. (2000) *Policy Research in Educational Settings: Contested Terrain*, Buckingham: Open University Press.

Parsons, W. (1995) *Public Policy: an Introduction to the Theory and Practice of Policy Analysis*, Aldershot: Edward Elgar.

Pratt, J. (1999) 'Testing policy' in J. Swann and J. Pratt (eds) *Improving Education: Realist Approaches to Method and Research*, London: Continuum.

Pratt, J. (2000) 'The emergence of the colleges' in A. Smithers and P. Robinson (eds) *Further Education Re-formed*, London: Falmer.

Qualifications and Curriculum Authority (QCA) (2004) *A Framework for Achievement: Recognising Qualifications and Skills in the 21st Century*, London: QCA.

Rainbird, H. (2003) 'Big on aspirations, weak on delivery' in NIACE 'Has the Government got it right?', *Adults Learning*, July 2003: 11–12.

Ranson, S. (1985) 'Contradictions in the government of educational change', *Political Studies*, 33 (1): 16–25.

Richardson, W., Woolhouse, J. and Finegold, D. (eds) (1993) *The Reform of Post-16 Education and Training in England and Wales*, Harlow: Longman.

Roberts, K. (2001) *Class in Modern Britain*, Basingstoke: Palgrove.

Schon, D. (1983) *The Reflective Practitioner*, New York: Basic Books.

Schon, D. (1987) *Educating the Reflective Practitioner: Towards a New Design for Teaching and Learning in the Professions*, San Francisco: Jossey Bass.

Schuller, T., Preston, J., Hammond, C., Bassett Grundy, A. and Bynner, J. (2004) *The Benefits of Learning: The Impact of Education on Heatlh, Family Life and Social Capital*, London: Routledge.

Sherlock, D. (2003) 'Mould-breaking' in NIACE 'Has the Government got it right?', *Adults Learning*, July 2003: 9–10.

Simon, H. A. (1957) *Models of Man: Social and Rational*, New York: John Wiley.

Skidmore, P. (2003) 'Beyond measure: why educational assessment is failing the test', Skidmore, Demos 2003 (available at www.demos.co.uk).

Smith, A. (2004) *Making Mathematics Count: The Report of Professor Adrian Smith's Inquiry into Post-14 Mathematics Education*, London: Stationery Office.

Smithers, A. and Robinson, P. (eds) (2000) *Further Education Re-formed*, London: Falmer Press.

Stanton, G. (2000) 'The new learning market: who pays, and what for', in FEDA *The New Learning Market*, London: FEDA.

Stasz, C., Hayward, G., Oh, S. and Wright, S. (2004) *Outcomes and Processes in Vocational Learning: A Review of the Literature*, London: Learning and Skills Research Centre.

Stasz, C. and Wright, S. (2004) *Emerging Policy for Vocational Learning in England: Will it Lead to a Better System?*, London: Learning and Skills Research Centre.

Taubman, D. (2000) 'Staff relations' in A. Smithers and P. Robinson (eds) *Further Education Re-formed*, London: Falmer Press.

Tett, L., Hamilton, M. and Hillier, Y. (eds) (2006) *Adult Literacy, Numeracy and Language: Policy, Practice and Research*, Maidenhead: McGraw Hill.

Tomlinson, M. (2004) *Final Report from the Tomlinson Working Group on 14–19 Reform*, London: DfES.

Wells, A. (2004) *Basic Skills Newsletter*, London: BSA.

Index

14–19 age group 36, 44, 66, 71, 73–76, 80, 85, 93, 99, 101–102, 106
  see also *14–19 Curriculum and Qualifications Reform* and *Final Report from the Tomlinson Working Group on 14–19 Reform*
14–19 Curriculum and Qualifications Reform: Final Report of the Working Group on 14–19 Reform (Foster Report) 2005 41, 78, 96, 98–100, 103, 107, 110
14–19 Education and Skills 2005 87

A level
  see qualifications
adult basic skills
  see basic skills
Adult Basic Skills and Strategy Unit (ABSSU) 56, 57, 62
adult education 22, 81, 83, 85, 87
Adult Education National Training Organisation (PAULO) 91
Adult Learning Inspectorate (ALI) 81, 84, 85, 88, 100
  Excalibur 84, 85, 88
adult literacy, language and numeracy (ALLN) 52, 53
  see also literacy, numeracy
Adults Learning Mathematics (ALM) 64

Advanced Certificate in Vocational Education (ACVE)
  see qualifications
Agenda for Change 2005 96–98, 103
agenda setting 4, 5, 6, 46
ambiguity 6, 14
apprenticeship 22, 25, 73
  Modern 42, 70, 71
Aristotle 2
assessment 55, 58, 60, 68–69, 73–74, 84
  self 86, 98
Association of Colleges (AoC) 101, 107

basic skills 38, 40, 42, 44, 46–47, 91, 102, 108
  of adults 13, 32, 37, 51–72, 100
  Agency 62, 63, 64
beacon status 41, 97
Bilston College 29
Blunkett, David 37, 59
Bureaucracy Task Force (BTF) 41

Cabinet Office 46
Callaghan, James (Jim) 23
capital investment 97, 98, 104
Centre for Excellence in Leadership (CEL) 40, 88, 105
Centre for Excellence in Teacher Training 92

Centre of Vocational Excellence (CoVE) 37–38, 92, 96
Certificate in Adult Literacy and Numeracy
  see qualifications
Certificate of Secondary Education (CSE)
  see qualifications
City and Guilds of London Institute 21, 40, 54, 89, 90, 91
  see also qualifications
Clarke, Charles 38
Colleges for Excellence and Innovation 2000 38,
colleges of higher education 23
competences 25–27, 68
comprehensive schools
  see schools
Confederation of British Industry (CBI) 42,
continuing professional development (CPD) 92
credit 75, 76
Credit and Qualifications Framework for Wales (CQFW) 76
critical discourse analysis
  see discourse
critical reflection 16–19, 48–50
Crowther Report 22
Curriculum 2000 71
cycles, policy 5–6, 11, 18

Department for Education and Skills (DfES) 7, 37, 39, 40, 42, 43, 56, 59, 61, 64, 85, 87, 88, 89, 94, 104, 107, 111
deliberative policy analysis (DPA) 9–10, 13, 15–17, 34, 48, 49
Department for Work and Pensions (DWP) 39, 43
Department of Education and Science (DES) 25, 43
Department of Trade and Industry (DTI) 39, 42, 43

Dewey, John 3
discourse 6, 9, 18, 48, 59, 62, 93, 98

Education Act 1870 21
Education Act 1944 22, 67
Education and Training for the Twenty-first Century 1991 27–28, 69
Education Maintenance Allowance (EMA) 42
Education Reform Act 1988 (ERA) 27, 82
employability 35, 38, 44
employers 22, 23, 26–28, 31, 33, 41–46, 49, 54, 62, 69, 75, 84, 88, 95, 97–98, 102–103, 111
Employment Department (ED) 25
Employment for the 1990s 1989 26
Employment Service 37
Employment Training (ET) 25
English for Speakers of Other Languages (ESOL) 54, 58, 91
Entry to Employment (E2E) 105
Europe 31, 79
  comparison with 26, 29, 42
  legislation 28
European Union (EU) 31, 53, 79
Excalibur
  see Adult Learning Inspectorate

fees 28, 42, 44, 45
Final Report from the Tomlinson Working Group on 14–19 Reform 2004 44, 71–75, 77–79
Forster Report 1870 20
Foster, Sir Andrew 96, 98
  Report see 14–19 Curriculum and Qualifications Reform
foundation degrees
  see qualifications
Framework for Achievement (FfA) 75–76, 78, 102

Framework for Regional
  Employment and Skills
  Action (FRESA) 43
franchises 28, 29
*Fresh Start: Improving Literacy and
  Numeracy, A* 1999 33, 52,
  53–54
Fryer, Sir Robert 31
funding 15, 17, 44, 47, 48, 54,
  55–56, 60, 62, 65, 96, 97, 99,
  102, 104, 108, 109,111
  mechanisms 28–34, 36–38,
    41–42, 45, 57, 63, 97–98,
    105
  see also fees, Further Education
    Funding Council, Learning
    and Skills Council
Further and Higher Education Act
  1992 28
  Schedule 2 28, 83
Further Education Development
  Agency (FEDA) 87
Further Education Funding
  Council (FEFC) 28, 29, 32,
  41, 82, 83, 86, 90, 97
Further Education National
  Training Organisation
  (FENTO) 40, 58, 60, 90–92
Further Education Staff College
  (FESC) 87
Further Education Unit (FEU) 87

'garbage can' approach (to
  policymaking) 5
General Certificate of Education
  (GCE)
  see qualifications
General Certificate of Secondary
  Education (GCSE)
  see qualifications
General National Vocational
  Qualification (GNVQ)
  see qualifications
Get On 57
grammar schools
  see schools

Green, Philip 96

Halton College 29
Her Majesty's Inspectorate (HMI)
  74, 81–82, 86
higher education 31, 32, 38, 44,
  69, 70, 72, 74, 75, 78, 100,
  106, 107
  see also universities
Hoyles, Professor Celia 61
human capital 93

implementation 4, 5–9, 13–14,
  17–18, 38, 46, 48, 56, 61,
  76–77, 80, 99, 103, 107, 111
individual learning account 31
Industrial Training Act 1964 22
Industrial Training Board (ITB) 25
industrial revolution 21
inspection 17, 34, 54, 60, Ch 6,
  99, 100, 106
  see also Adult Literacy
    Inspectorate, Office for
    Standards in Education
Institute for Learning (IfL) 92
International Adult Literacy
  Survey (IALS)
  see OECD

Jobcentre Plus 88
Johnson, Alan 39

Kelly, Ruth 74, 79, 102–103, 107
Kennedy, Helena 31

Lasswell, Harold 3
learndirect 31, 56, 57, 58,
Learning Age, The 1998 31
Learning and Skills Act 2000
  36–37, 38, 87, 107
Learning and Skills Council 15,
  17, 18, 32, 36, 37, 41, 43, 63,
  75, 94, 96–97, 102
  inspection 81–83, 88, 96
  local LSCs 39, 43, 45,106

National Learner Satisfaction
Survey 104
Learning and Skills Development
Agency (LSDA) 44, 64,
87–88
Learning and Skills Research
Centre 77, 87–88
Learning Partnerships 36
Learning to Succeed 1998 32, 35, 36,
38
Learning Works 1997 31
Leitch, Sir Sandy 78, 96
see also Skills for the Global
Economy
lifelong learning 31–33, 36, 42, 46,
48, 53, 63, 103, 104,
108–109
Lifelong Learning Sector Skills
Council (LLUK) 40, 91
life skills
see skills
Lisbon Strategy 79
Literacy and Language Unit 59
local education authority (LEA)
23, 24, 27, 28, 81–82, 94,
109, 110
London College of Fashion 96
London Working Men's
Association 21

Manpower Services Commission
(MSC) 25
mechanics' institutes 21
Memorandum on Lifelong Learning
(EU) 31, 53
Modern Apprenticeship
see apprenticeship
Morris, Estelle 71
Moser, Sir Claus 32, 52, 53
report see Fresh Start, A

National Advisory Group for
Continuing Education and
Lifelong Learning
(NAGCELL) 33

National Association of Teachers
in Further and Higher
Education (NATFHE) 82
National Audit Office 57, 60
National Certificates 22, 23
National Child Development
Study (NCDS) 52
National Council for Vocational
Qualifications (NCVQ)
25
national curriculum 54, 56–58,
64, 70
for adult basic skills 13, 56
National Employer Training
Programme (NETP) 44–45,
97
National Institute for Adult and
Continuing Education
(NIACE) 102
National Learner Satisfaction
Survey
see Learning and Skills Council
National Open College Network
(NOCN) 70, 75
National Professional
Qualification for Headship
(NPQH)
see qualifications
National Research and
Development Centre for
Adult Literacy, Numeracy
and ESOL (NRDC) 59, 62,
64
national training organization
(NTO) 90, 91
National Vocational Qualification
(NVQ)
see qualifications
National Skills Task Force 33
National Skills Task Force: Towards a
National Skills Agenda 33
New Training Initiative: Programme
for Action, A 1981 25, 68
non-advanced further education
(NAFE) 23

Northern Ireland Credit
  Accumulation and Transfer
  Scheme (NICATS) 76

Office for Standards in Education
  (Ofsted) 39, 58, 60, 81, 83,
  85, 86, 88, 100
On the Move 51
Organisation for Economic
  Cooperation and
  Development (OECD) 31,
  53
  International Adult Literacy
    Survey (IALS) 31, 53
  Programme for International
    Student Assessment
    (PISA) 31

participation
  rates 26, 29, 70, 78
  widening 31, 33, 36–38, 42, 54,
    63, 105, 108
partnership 31, 35, 37, 38, 42, 45
  see also Learning Partnerships
performance
  indicators 15, 27, 37, 47, 82
  see also targets
  measurement 17, 78
pluralism 8
polytechnics 23, 24
Popper, Karl 11
Programme for International
  Student Attainment (PISA)
  see OECD
Public Service Agreement (PSA)
  78, 105, 106

qualifications 3, 8, 15, 16, 27, 29,
    30, 41, 47, 57, 63, 65, Ch 5,
  Advanced Certificate in
    Vocational Education
    (ACVE) 71
  Advanced Subsidiary level (AS) 71
  basic skills 47, 54, 56, 62, 102
  Certificate in Adult Literacy and
    Numeracy 57

Certificate of Secondary
  Education (CSE) 67, 68
City and Guilds Teaching
  Certificate 90, 91
Fashion Retail Diploma 96
foundation degrees 44
General Certificate of
  Education (GCE)
  *A level 23, 24, 67–71, 73–79,
    96*
  O level 67, 68, 76
General Certificate of
  Secondary Education
  (GCSE) 44, 56, 57, 62, 68–
  70, 73, 74–75, 78–79
General National Vocational
  Qualification (GNVQ) 69,
  71
ICT 62, 106
level 2 22, 42, 102
level 3 44, 58, 103
level 4 58
national framework 3, 34, 35,
  56, 102
National Professional
  Qualification for Headship
  (NPQH) 40
National Vocational
  Qualification (NVQ) 68,
  70, 71, 80
reform 33, 43–44, 98–99
Royal Society of Arts 90
for teachers 40, 54, 55, 58, 60,
  64, 89–92, 103
vocational 23, 25–26, 28, 40, 56
qualified teacher status (QTS) 40,
  91
Qualified Teacher Learning and
  Skills status (QTLS) 92
Qualifications and Curriculum
  Authority (QCA) 71, 75, 79,
  94
Qualifying for Success 1997 71
Quality Improvement Agency
  (QIA) 88–89, 98

rationality (in policymaking) 3–4,
    10–12
*Realising our Potential: Individuals,
    Employers, Nation* 33, 39,
    41–46
*Realizing the Potential: A Review of
    the Future Role of Further
    Education Colleges* 99
Research and Practice in Adult
    Literacy (RaPAL) 64
Robbins Report 1963 23
Royal Society of Arts (RSA) 21,
    90
    see also qualifications

schools 6, 24, 28, 31, 32, 36, 40,
    41, 46, 51, 54, 67–72, 82, 91,
    95, 102–103, 107
    comprehensive 24
    grammar 22, 24, 67
    secondary modern 22, 24, 67
    specialist 78
    technical 22, 24
    see also sixth form
Scotland 108
Scottish Credit and Qualifications
    Framework (SCQF) 76
secondary modern schools
    see schools
Sector Skills Agreements 45
Sector Skills Councils 35, 40, 91
self-assessment
    see assessment
sixth form 23, 28, 32, 36, 67, 71,
    78, 105
    colleges 24, 71
skills
    Academies 45, 95–96
    Alliance 41, 42
    centres 25
    life 26
    training 26
    see also basic skills, Learning and
        Skills Council, National
        Skills Task Force, Sector
        Skills Agreements, Sector

    Skills Councils, Skills for
        Life strategy
Skills and Education Network
    (SENET) 49
Skills for Life strategy (SK4L) 32,
    46, 47, Ch 4, 78
    Unit 56, 62–63, 64
*Skills: Getting on in Business,
    Getting on at Work* 33
Skills for the Global Economy 2005
    100, 103
Small Business Council 42
social capital 8
social exclusion 33–34, 35, 51–52,
    53
social inclusion
    see social exclusion
Society of Arts
    see Royal Society of Arts 21, 90
stagist approaches (to
    policymaking) 5–7, 48
Standards Unit 39, 40, 49, 63, 64
staying on
    see participation
Stubbs, Sir William 71
Strategic Areas Review (StAR) 39,
    105
Success for All 33, Ch 3, 88,
    104–107
systems approaches (to policy) 7–8,
    13

Tackling the Adult Skills Gap 33
targets 7, 29, 32, 33, 34, 37, 41,
    46–48, 49, 55–57, 60, 61,
    62, 63, 77–78, 88–89, 102,
    105–106
    groups 22, 33, 40, 55, 65
teacher training 39, 40, 58, 91–92,
    105
Technical and Vocational
    Education Initiative (TVEI)
    70
technical education 21–23, 38
technical schools
    see schools

Technical Instruction Act 1889 21
tertiary colleges 24, 28
Tomlinson, Sir Mike 71
  Report *see Final Report from the Tomlinson Working Group on 14–19 Reform*
Trades Union Congress (TUC) 42
Training and Enterprise Councils (TECs) 27–29, 31, 32, 70
Training Opportunities Scheme (TOPS) 25, 26
Treasury 39, 45, 46

unemployment 23–26, 37, 43, 52, 68, 76, 79
universities 23, 24, 32, 46, 61, 67, 68, 74, 77, 79
  South Bank 58
  University for Industry (UfI) 31

see also higher education

vocational qualifications
  see qualifications
vocationalism 26, 27
voluntary initiative 21, 22, 43
voluntary organizations 31, 42
volunteers 51

Wales 20, 108
Wells, Alan 62
whisky money 21
Working Together: Education and Training 1986 25

Youth Opportunities Scheme (YOPS) 25, 26
Youth Training Scheme (YTS) 25, 26, 68